200 thirty-minute meals

hamlyn | all color cookbook

200 thirty-minute meals

An Hachette UK Company
www.hachette.co.uk

First published in Great Britain in 2010 by
Hamlyn, a division of Octopus Publishing Group Ltd
Endeavour House
189 Shaftesbury Avenue
London
WC2H 8JY
www.octopusbooksusa.com

Distributed in the U.S. and Canada by Octopus Books USA:
c/o Hachette Book Group
237 Park Avenue
New York, NY 10017

ISBN 978-0-600-62163-8

Printed and bound in China

2 3 4 5 6 7 8 9 10

Standard level spoon measurements are used in all recipes.
1 tablespoon = one 15 ml spoon
1 teaspoon = one 5 ml spoon

Ovens should be preheated to the specified temperature—if
using a fan-assisted oven, follow the manufacturer's
instructions for adjusting the time and the temperature.

Fresh herbs should be used unless otherwise stated.

Medium eggs should be used unless otherwise stated.

The Food and Drug Administration advises that eggs should
not be consumed raw. This book contains some dishes made
with raw or lightly cooked eggs. It is prudent for vulnerable
people, such as pregnant and nursing mothers, invalids, the
elderly, babies, and young children, to avoid uncooked or
lightly cooked dishes made with eggs. Once prepared, these
dishes should be kept refrigerated and used promptly.

This book includes dishes made with nuts and nut derivatives. It
is advisable for those with known allergic reactions to nuts and
nut derivatives and those who may be potentially vulnerable to
these allergies, such as pregnant and nursing mothers, invalids,
the elderly, babies, and children, to avoid dishes made with nuts
and nut oils. It is also prudent to check the labels of prepared
ingredients for the possible inclusion of nut derivatives.

contents

introduction

introduction

Most families' lives are packed with activity. Not only do many parents have to juggle their work with child care, but their spare time is often taken up with activities that fulfill their own and their children's physical, creative, and social needs. Children, too, have busy and varied lives. Even after school it's likely that the rest of the day will be a busy round of being dropped off at ballet class or baseball practice or being collected from swimming classes or drum or judo practice. Then there's barely time to get everybody fed and the young ones into bed before it's time for the adults to put up their feet and have a quiet glass of wine.

When we stop to think about our modern lives, it's easy to see how meals can get pushed into the background and be made to fit around our other commitments. Time is in such short supply that most of us scarcely have time to eat our meals, let alone plan them, shop for them, and cook them. That is why we have included the delicious recipes in this book. All of them can be prepared in under 30 minutes and many of them can be prepared and cooked in that time. When you spend less time in the kitchen, you will have more time to savor and enjoy both your food and the company of your family and friends.

the benefits of family meals

Many of us are guilty of grabbing supper as we are on the way to a meeting, or we let the

children perch on stools at the kitchen counter to wolf down a bowl of something hot before they set off to do something else.

However, we should all remember the huge benefits that accrue to both ourselves and our children if we sit down together as a family around the dining table to eat a proper meal. This is not only important from the nutritional point of view, but is also a major part of growing up and one that most of us can remember from our own childhoods.

Mealtimes should be significant social events for families. They give us an opportunity to talk to each other about what has happened during the day without the sound of a television set in the background distracting our attention. They also give us a chance to be good role models for our children. Eating together enables us to encourage the children to try out new foods, as well as make sure that they have healthier versions of the foods they love. Sitting down to eat a meal in a structured, sensitive, and loving environment also gives children an opportunity to learn good tablemanners—something we all hope and assume they will learn by the time they reach adulthood.

In addition, when you eat meals sitting down at a table, your body will be able to get more nutrients from the food you are eating. So switch off the television and set the table.

being prepared

Although most people recognize the benefits of providing well-cooked and well-presented meals, they often fail in the preparation of family meals. You may have great plans for a sit-down meal, but if it takes a long time to prepare, the time you spend eating and enjoying it is minimal and undermines your good intentions. So we have come up with this selection of quick-and-easy recipes. Some of these dishes are already well-known family favorites, but others we hope will become new regulars in your family. Not only are they all surprisingly quick to prepare, but they are also highly nutritious and taste wonderful.

The key to a successful family meal lies in the planning. If you know you have a busy week ahead, try to find time to sit down the week before and plan your meals and write a shopping list. If time is really tight, consider using online shopping services. Although there is a delivery fee, you will save a huge amount of time when you don't have to walk around the supermarket and handle the products yourself. All you have to do is transfer the shopping to your cabinets when it's been delivered. Internet food shopping can save you hours each month.

key ingredients

Even when you have spent time making plans, sometimes things change at the last minute, and you may find that you have no time at all to prepare something from nothing. For this reason, it's a good idea to keep some key ingredients in your pantry just for emergencies.

9

There are some basic foodstuffs that you will always need. These include staple carbohydrates, such as rice and pasta (ideally brown if you can buy it), couscous, noodles, and rolled oats.

Even when you have no fresh meat, if you have a bag of cashew nuts and a store of canned tuna, salmon, and beans in the pantry, some eggs in the refrigerator, and a bag of frozen shrimp in the freezer, you can still provide a nutritious protein-based dinner in a matter of minutes.

To add flavor and to help the cooking process, make sure you always have some chicken and vegetable stock cubes or granules and soy sauce, together with olive, sesame oil and canola oil, salt and black

pepper and tomato and sundried tomato paste. You should also have some key herbs and spices, such as mixed herbs, allspice, Chinese five-spice powder, ground cinnamon, coriander, cumin, and nutmeg and chili sauce or flakes.

Other produce you should keep to help you create some last-minute sauces include flour, cornstarch, canned tomatoes, tomato sauce, passata, olives, sharp cheddar cheese and some nonfat dry milk powder. And for emergency desserts keep sugar, honey, maple syrup, a couple of cans of fruit, and some graham crackers in the pantry and some vanilla ice cream, fruit sorbet, and waffles in the freezer.

Crème fraîche and plain yogurt can be used in both savory and sweet dishes, but these ingredients have a short shelf life and should ideally be included in your regular shopping.

Although it's not a good idea to rely on store-bought sauces, which are often made with unnecessary preservatives and colorings, it is useful to have a jar or two of good-quality green or red pesto in your pantry. You can spread a little pesto over baked chicken or fish or stir it through pasta for a quick and delicious lunch. The best-quality pesto is made with only basil, Parmesan cheese, pine nuts, and olive oil, and it's easy to make in a food processor from scratch yourself, but when time is limited a good ready-made version is one of the best "chef's cheats" you can buy.

short cuts

With a great selection of basic ingredients in your kitchen pantry, a little time spent planning your weekly meals and your shopping delivered to your door, you are nearly ready to get down to feeding your hungry family this week. But before you do so, try to fit in a few small jobs the next time you find yourself with some spare minutes. They will save time later and help take some of the fuss out of preparing good-quality, nutritious meals.

When bread starts to turn stale, don't throw it away or put it on the compost. Instead, put it in the food processor and make bread crumbs. Bag them up and store them in the freezer for the next time you're making breaded chicken nuggets or need a crunchy topping for an ovenbake.

Shred cheddar and grate Parmesan cheese and freeze them in small portions ready for use in sauces and risottos. Keep ginger and chilies in your freezer. You can grate ginger when it's still frozen straight into your recipe. Chilies need a few minutes to thaw before they are ready for chopping. Buy chopped frozen spinach, which can be added to dishes straight from the freezer.

When you make a soup, stew, curry, or ragout-style sauce, make double the quantity specified in the recipe and store the surplus in your freezer. When you need to create an emergency meal, it is amazing what you will be able to find in your freezer to save the day.

If you do not have a microwave and have forgotten to take meat, poultry, or fish out of the freezer, you can speed up the process by immersing the wrapped frozen food in a sink of cold water and letting it stand for a couple of hours.

Instead of crushing garlic, chop the end off a clove and grate it instead. It saves time washing up the garlic press and wastes less of the clove. If the recipe requires a large number of garlic cloves, you can save time by adding garlic paste straight from the tube. The flavor is intense, so be careful: you need only a small amount to replace a clove of garlic.

If you have some heavy cream left over, pour it into ice-cube trays and freeze it. You can then remove as little or as much as you need for the next recipe that requires it.

Fresh cilantro is a wonderful herb that adds huge amounts of flavor to all kinds of dishes. Make sure you always have the flavor of cilantro by keeping a supply of pots or tubes of cilantro paste, which preserves the leaves in a mixture of oil and vinegar. Alternatively, freeze a bunch of fresh cilantro in a plastic bag ready to crumble into your cooking. Freezing will blacken the leaves and marginally reduce the flavor, but it is still preferable to having no cilantro at all.

Slice bread before you freeze it. You can then remove only the amount you require. Similarly, cut muffins in half before freezing them so you can take them straight from the freezer and put them under the broiler for toasting.

fast food that's good food

Whether you are young or old, a vegetarian or an omnivore, we all need much the same nutrients from the food we eat. Our energy comes from food and fluids, and if we are to get the full and complete range of nutrients that our bodies need, we should be consuming carbohydrates, protein, fats, fiber,

and water as well as a variety of vitamins and minerals. These nutrients not only fuel our bodies, but many of them also actually improve our health and help protect us against diseases. If we eat well, we feel well, our mood is improved, and we can cope better with stress—which can only be a good thing if we're running a busy household.

Just because time is limited does not mean that we can't eat healthily. Fast food can still be good, nutritious, and healthy food, as many of the recipes in this book prove. The secret is to mix up the dishes and get the family eating as great a variety of foods as possible, so that everyone gets all the nutrition they need and a chance to eat their favorite food at some point in the week. If one child hates beans but loves red meat, while the other hates red meat but loves omelets, so be it. You may not be able to please the whole family in one sitting, but if you mix up the recipes, everyone will have at least one meal a week that they really love, and you will avoid falling into a "meal rut," when you eat the same foods day after day.

In the second chapter of this book, Pasta, Rice & Noodles, the recipes are based on a range of carbohydrates. Although carbs have had a bad press in recent years, good carbohydrates (otherwise known as complex carbohydrates) are actually vital to our health and should form the basis of every healthy diet. Complex carbohydrates include grains, bread, rice, and pasta as well as fresh fruit and vegetables, legumes, and dairy products.

Fresh fruits and vegetables are not every child's favorite food, but they should form the basis of every meal and should also, ideally, be your first choice for snacks. They are packed with antioxidants, which protect us against disease, and contain vitamins and minerals, such as iron and calcium, to make our bodies work properly. For this reason, fruit and vegetables feature in many of the recipes in this book. They will add important vitamins and minerals to your diet and give your food a great flavor and color.

Pasta, rice, and noodles are firm favorites in the Western diet, and this isn't surprising because they are a great base to which can be added a host of intoxicating flavors. Whenever you can, choose brown or whole-grain versions because the nutrients have not been processed out of them and they retain their fiber content.

Fiber is found only in plant-based foods, and it is vital for the health of the whole family. First, fiber keeps the gut healthy and aids digestion, and second, fibrous foods help to maintain our blood-sugar levels. Fiber takes longer to digest than other types of foods, helping to make you feel fuller for longer, which helps overcome the temptation of snacking on unhealthy, fatty foods between meals.

Legumes are another good source of fiber, and they feature in several tasty dishes in the One Pot and Vegetarian chapters. Persuading your family to eat legumes will benefit everybody. They are a good source of protein, are full of B vitamins, calcium, and iron, are low in saturated fat and are cholesterol free. Teenage girls especially, who often go through phases of faddy eating or experiment with vegetarianism, have an increased need for iron and will benefit if there are more legumes in their diet. Let them try Braised Lentils with Gremolata (see pages 196–97) or Chorizo and Chickpea Stew (see pages 138–39). Or you could spoil the whole family by cooking the Sausage and Bean Casserole (see pages 88–89), which is real comfort food for a wintry day.

encouraging fussy eaters
Children young and old can be notoriously fussy eaters, and many seem to be able to exist on pasta, cheese sandwiches, and little else. But if you want your children to develop healthy eating habits and you are eager to cook and share family meals together, it is vital that your children learn to like and accept new and different tastes. Cooking twice in one evening, once for the children and once for the adults, not only is exhausting, but also allows the children to develop picky and fussy eating habits, because they are able to demand their favorites night after night.

If your children are typical, getting them to eat protein probably won't be a problem. Many of the Meaty Treats in the fourth chapter are real family classics, and few children (or adults) will be able to resist Sausages with Mustard Mash (see pages 116–17). Sweet and Sour Pork (see pages 132–33) is an absolute winner with adults and children alike.

Getting younger children to eat fish and seafood can be more difficult, but try Roast Cod and Olive Risotto (see pages 164–65) or Angler fish Kebabs (see pages 170–71), and you will be pleasantly surprised to see the whole family wolf down their fish and ask for more.

trying new foods
When you cook for the whole family so that everyone eats together, you will start to encourage your children to try new tastes and textures. Start simply. Suggest to the family that one day in the week is the day to try new foods—"Trying Tuesdays," for example—and reward younger children who eat something new with a sticker or star chart. Older children can be allowed to stay up for 10 minutes later in the evening.

Present the meal in serving bowls in the center of the table and encourage children to help themselves. This will help them feel they have some control over what is put on their plates, and they will be more inclined to eat it. Do not bribe children with food, and never force a child to eat something they clearly don't like. A bad experience at the dinner table will stay in a child's memory for a long time, and they will associate negative feelings with that food for months or even years afterward.

On days when you are offering new foods, avoid snacks close to dinner time so that

everyone will be hungry before their meal. If you do this there is a greater chance that fussy eaters will eat whatever is presented to them. If a child continually refuses their food, make sure that they are not drinking too much fruit juice or are snacking between meals, both of which can take away the appetite.

Never prepare an alternative if a child refuses the meal you have cooked. This only encourages fussy behavior and will slowly erode your enjoyment of cooking for your family.

Be aware that children have sensitive taste buds, so be cautious when you are adding exotic and spicy flavors. When you are preparing a curry, for example, it may be wise to let your children get used to the more exotic flavors within the meal before adding any chili.

eating together

Remember that when a family eats together you have an opportunity to be a wonderful role model for your children. If you love curry, they will secretly want to like curry, too, so keep cooking new dishes and keep offering young children a lot of encouragement. In time, by making mealtimes fun, interesting, and happy social events, you will discover that your children will happily eat all kinds of different flavors, textures, and dishes, and you will regularly be able to enjoy good, healthy food together as a family.

So get cooking and start creating some wonderful mealtime memories.

snacks &
light bites

minestrone soup

Serves **4**
Preparation time **5 minutes**
Cooking time **25 minutes**

2 tablespoons **olive oil**
1 **onion**, diced
1 **garlic clove**, crushed
2 **celery stalks**, chopped
1 **leek**, finely sliced
1 **carrot**, chopped
13 oz can **chopped tomatoes**
2½ cups **chicken stock** or
    vegetable stock
1 **zucchini**, diced
½ small **green cabbage**,
    shredded
1 **bay leaf**
⅓ cup canned **cannellini
    beans**
3 oz **spaghetti**, broken into
    small pieces, or small pasta
    shapes
1 tablespoon chopped
    flat-leaf parsley
salt and **black pepper**
½ cup freshly grated
    Parmesan cheese, to serve

Heat the oil in a large saucepan. Add the onion, garlic, celery, leek, and carrot and sauté over medium heat, stirring occasionally, for 3 minutes.

Add the tomatoes, stock, zucchini, cabbage, bay leaf, and cannellini beans. Bring to a boil, then lower the heat and simmer for 10 minutes.

Add the spaghetti and season to taste with salt and black pepper. Stir well and cook for an additional 8 minutes. Keep stirring, otherwise the soup may stick to the bottom of the pan.

Add the chopped parsley just before serving, and stir well. Ladle into warmed soup bowls and serve with grated Parmesan.

For bacon & lentil soup, fry 6 slices roughly chopped bacon with the onion, garlic, and vegetables and then add ⅓ cup red lentils with the tomatoes, stock, and cannellini beans. Simmer for 20 minutes, until the lentils make the soup thicken naturally. Omit the pasta. Serve in warmed serving bowls with 1 tablespoon chopped parsley stirred through and ½ cup grated Parmesan cheese sprinkled over.

summer vegetable soup

Serves **4**
Preparation time **10 minutes**
Cooking time **20 minutes**

1 teaspoon **olive oil**
1 **leek**, thinly sliced
1 large **potato**, chopped
3 cups prepared **mixed
  summer vegetables**, such
  as peas, asparagus spears,
  fava beans, and zucchini
2 tablespoons chopped **mint**,
  plus extra leaves to garnish
3¾ cups **vegetable stock**
2 tablespoons **crème fraîche**
  or **Greek yogurt**
salt (optional) and **black
  pepper**

Heat the oil in a medium saucepan, add the leek and potato, and cook for 3–4 minutes, until softened.

Add the mixed vegetables to the pan with the mint and stock and bring to a boil. Reduce the heat and simmer for 10 minutes.

Transfer the soup to a blender or food processor and blend until smooth. Return the soup to the pan and season with salt, if necessary, and black pepper to taste. Heat through and serve in warmed bowls with the crème fraiche swirled over the top. Garnish with extra mint leaves.

For vegetable soup with cheesy croutons, cook 1 leek and 1 large potato as above, add 3¾ cups vegetable stock, and bring to a boil. Cook for 10 minutes, then transfer to a food processor or blender and process until smooth. Return to the pan and add another ⅓ cup stock, all the remaining vegetables, roughly chopped, and 2 tablespoons chopped mint. Cook for an additional 10 minutes. Meanwhile, thinly slice a thin French baguette, cover the slices with shredded cheddar cheese, and broil under a preheated hot broiler for 5 minutes, until golden and bubbling. Serve the soup in warmed serving bowls with the cheesy toast on top.

chicken noodle soup

Serves **4**
Preparation time **10 minutes**
Cooking time **12 minutes**

5 cups **chicken stock**
1 **star anise**
3 inch piece of **cinnamon stick**, broken up
2 **garlic cloves**, finely chopped
2 tablespoons **Thai fish sauce**
8 **cilantro roots**, finely chopped
4 teaspoons **light brown sugar**
4 teaspoons **light soy sauce**
7 oz boneless, skinless **chicken breast**, cut into cubes
1½ cups **green vegetables**, such as cabbage, Swiss chard, or bok choy, roughly chopped
¾ cup **bean sprouts**
7 oz **straight-to-wok rice noodles**
⅓ cup fresh **cilantro leaves**

Put the chicken stock, star anise, cinnamon stick, garlic, fish sauce, cilantro roots, sugar, and soy sauce into a large saucepan and bring slowly to a boil.

Add the chicken and simmer gently for 4 minutes.

Add the green vegetables and bean sprouts and simmer for 2 minutes.

Divide the noodles between 4 bowls, pour over the soup, and sprinkle the cilantro leaves on top.

For coconut & chicken soup, replace 1⅔ cups of the chicken stock with canned coconut milk. Cook the stock, herbs and spices, sugar, and fish and soy sauces, and chicken as above, simmering the green vegetables and bean sprouts for 2 minutes and adding 2 cups shredded snow peas for the final 1 minute of cooking for extra crunch. Ladle into warmed serving bowls over noodles as above and garnish with fresh cilantro leaves.

croque monsieur

Serves **4**
Preparation time **10 minutes**
Cooking time **10 minutes**

7 tablespoons **butter**,
   softened
8 slices of **white bread**
4 slices of **cheddar cheese**
4 slices of cooked **ham**
¼ cup **vegetable oil**
black pepper

Spread half the butter over one side of each slice of bread. Put a slice of cheddar on 4 of the buttered slices, top with a slice of ham, and sprinkle with black pepper. Top with the remaining slices of bread, butter side down, and press down hard.

Melt half the rest of the butter with half the oil in a large skillet, and fry 2 croques until golden brown, turning once. Cook the remaining 2 in the same way.

For croque madames, prepare the croque monsieurs as above but omit the cheese. Heat ¼ cup vegetable oil in a skillet and cook the ham sandwiches until they are golden and warm. Remove from the skillet and keep warm. Add another 1 tablespoon oil to the skillet and break 4 eggs into the pan. Cook until the white is firm but the yolk is still soft. Transfer the warm ham sandwiches to warmed serving plates and use a spatula to lay an egg on top of each. Garnish with chopped flat-leaf parsley to serve.

homemade pigs in a blanket

Makes **15**
Preparation time **15 minutes**,
 plus chilling
Cooking time **15 minutes**

13 oz good-quality **sausages**
1⅔ cups **all-purpose flour**,
 plus extra for dusting
⅓ cup **whole-wheat flour**
½ cup plus 2 tablespoons
 (1¼ sticks) **butter**, chilled
 and diced
3 tablespoons **iced water**
1 tablespoon **poppy seeds**
1 **egg**, beaten

Snip each sausage at one end and squeeze the sausage meat out onto a cutting board lightly dusted with flour. Roll out into thinner sausages.

Sift both flours and the salt into a bowl. Add the butter and rub it in with the fingertips until the mixture resembles fine bread crumbs. Add enough of the measured iced water to mix to a soft dough, then stir in the poppy seeds. Turn the dough out on to a lightly floured surface and knead briefly.

Roll the pastry out on a well-floured surface to a rectangle measuring 12 x 10 inches, then cut into three 4 x 10 inch strips. Lay the sausage meat down the center of each strip. Brush 1 edge of each strip with beaten egg, roll over, and flute the edges. Cut each strip into five 2 inch sausage rolls and put on a baking sheet.

Make a couple of cuts in the top of each roll and brush with the remaining egg. Refrigerate for 15 minutes before baking in a preheated oven, 400°F, for 15 minutes. Remove from the oven and let cool before lifting off the sheet.

For roasted vegetable & pigs in a blanket, core, seed, and roughly chop 1 small red and 1 small yellow bell pepper and chop 1 medium zucchini. Toss the vegetables with 1 tablespoon olive oil and roast on a baking sheet in a preheated oven, 400°F, for 30 minutes, until softened. Let cool. Combine the vegetables with 10 oz sausage meat. Roll out the pastry, then use the stuffing to make 15 sausage rolls. Bake as above.

goat cheese omelets

Serves **4**
Preparation time **10 minutes**
Cooking time **20 minutes**

¼ cup **olive oil**
1 lb **cherry tomatoes** (mixed red and yellow), halved
a little chopped **basil**
12 **eggs**
2 tablespoons **whole-grain mustard**
4 tablespoons **butter**
3½ oz **soft goat cheese**, diced
salt and **black pepper**
watercress, to garnish

Heat the oil in a skillet and fry the tomatoes (you may have to do this in 2 batches) for 2–3 minutes, until they have softened. Add the basil and season with salt and black pepper, then transfer to a bowl and keep warm.

Beat the eggs with the mustard and season with salt and black pepper.

Melt a quarter of the butter in an omelet pan or small skillet until it stops foaming, then swirl in a quarter of the egg mixture. Fork over the omelet so that it cooks evenly. As soon as it is set on the bottom (but still a little runny in the middle), dot over a quarter of the goat cheese and cook for an additional 30 seconds. Carefully slide the omelet onto a warmed plate, folding it in half as you do so.

Repeat with the remaining mixture to make 3 more omelets. Serve with the tomatoes and garnish with watercress.

For chorizo, plum tomato & chili omelets, cut 6 large plum tomatoes into quarters and fry them in ¼ cup olive oil. Add 7½ oz thinly sliced chorizo sausage and 1 teaspoon chopped fresh chili. Cook for an additional minute until lightly browned. Beat and cook the eggs as above, but omit the goat cheese. Serve the omelets with the chorizo mixture, garnished with arugula leaves.

blt sandwich

Serves **1**
Preparation time **5 minutes**
Cooking time **10 minutes**

2 lean **bacon** slices
2 slices of **whole-grain bread**
  or **multigrain bread**
2 tablespoons **mayonnaise**
2 **tomatoes**, halved
about 4 **baby lettuce leaves**
salt and **black pepper**

Heat a small, nonstick skillet and cook the bacon, turning once, until it is golden brown and crisp. Remove and drain on paper towels.

Toast the bread on both sides. Spread one side of each piece of toast with mayonnaise and arrange the bacon, tomatoes, and lettuce on top of one of the pieces. Season with salt and black pepper and top with the other piece of toast. Cut into quarters. Serve hot or cold.

For a toasted breakfast sandwich, cook the bacon as above. Cook 2 thick pork sausages until golden and cooked through. Slice the sausages lengthwise into 3 long, thin slices and set aside to keep warm. In a separate, medium skillet, heat 1 tablespoon vegetable oil. Beat 2 eggs and cook over moderate heat for 1–2 minutes, until just set. Arrange the bacon and sausages on a slice of warm toast. Cut the egg into quarters and arrange on top. Season with black pepper and scatter over chopped parsley. Spread a little ketchup on the other slice of toast and top the sandwich. Cut into quarters and serve warm.

chicken dippers with salsa

Serves **4**
Preparation time **20 minutes**
Cooking time **6–8 minutes**

2 **eggs**
2 tablespoons **milk**
2 cups **fresh bread crumbs**
¼ cup freshly grated
  Parmesan cheese
3 boneless, skinless **chicken
  breasts**, about 1 lb in total,
  cut into long, fingerlike slices
2 tablespoons **butter**
2 tablespoons **vegetable oil**
salt and **black pepper**

Salsa
2 **tomatoes**, diced
¼ **cucumber**, diced
⅓ cup canned or ½ cup frozen
  corn kernals, defrosted if
  frozen
1 tablespoon fresh **cilantro
  leaves**, chopped

Put the salsa ingredients in a bowl and mix together.

Beat the eggs, milk, and a little salt and black pepper together in a bowl.

Mix the bread crumbs with the Parmesan.

Dip one chicken strip into the egg, then roll in the bread crumbs. Carry on doing this until all the chicken strips are well covered.

Heat the butter and oil in a large skillet and add the chicken strips. Cook for 6–8 minutes, turning a few times, until they are brown all over. Serve with the salsa to dip into.

For salmon nuggets with a minty dip, cut 1 lb salmon fillets into strips. Mix 2 tablespoons chopped parsley with 2 cups fresh bread crumbs and coat each piece of salmon in the mixture. Cook the fish in butter and oil as above for 2–3 minutes, until it is cooked and the bread crumbs are golden, being careful not to break the fish when turning. Mix 1½ cups plain yogurt with ¼ cup chopped mint leaves and 3 tablespoons finely diced cucumber. Serve the salmon with the dip in a separate bowl.

caesar salad

Serves **4**
Preparation time **20 minutes**
Cooking time **5 minutes**

1 **garlic clove**, peeled and
  crushed
4 **anchovy fillets** in oil,
  drained and chopped
juice of **1 lemon**
1–2 teaspoons **mustard**
1 **egg yolk**
1 cup **olive oil**
vegetable oil, for frying
3 slices of **white bread**, cut
  into cubes
1 **romaine lettuce**, washed
  and torn into pieces
3 tablespoons freshly grated
  Parmesan cheese
black pepper

Put the garlic, anchovies, lemon juice, mustard, and egg yolk in a small bowl and sprinkle with black pepper. Mix well until combined. Slowly drizzle in the olive oil, mixing all the time to make a thick creamy sauce. If the sauce is too thick, add a little water.

Heat the vegetable oil in a skillet. Test with one of the bread cubes to see if it is hot enough; if the bread sizzles, add the rest of the cubes, turning them when they are golden brown, then drain on paper towels.

Put the lettuce into a large bowl, pour over the dressing, and sprinkle with 2 tablespoons of the Parmesan; mix well. Sprinkle on the croutons and the rest of the Parmesan and serve.

For bacon salad with walnuts & croutons, make a dressing by mixing ¼ cup homemade mayonnaise with 2 tablespoons white wine vinegar and 1 teaspoon Dijon mustard. Broil 6 bacon slices until crisp and cut into pieces. Toss the bacon with the torn leaves of 1 romaine lettuce and ½ cup toasted walnut pieces. Make croutons with whole-grain bread. Assemble the salad by tossing the ingredients together and drizzling over the mustard mayonnaise.

hot thai beef salad

Serves **4**
Preparation time **15 minutes**
Cooking time: **5–10 minutes**

2 tablespoons **vegetable oil**
1 lb **round steak** or **beef
tenderloin**, cut into thin
strips across the grain
3 **garlic cloves**, finely
chopped
2 **green chilies**, seeded if
desired, thinly sliced
½ cup **lemon juice**
1 tablespoon **Thai fish sauce**
2 teaspoons **superfine sugar**
2 ripe **papayas**, peeled and
thinly sliced
½ large **cucumber**, cut into
matchsticks
¾ cup **bean sprouts**
1 **crisp lettuce**, shredded
chili sauce, to serve (optional)

Heat the oil in a wok over moderate heat. Add the
steak, garlic, and chilies, increase the heat to high, and
stir-fry for 3–4 minutes, or until the steak is browned
on all sides. Pour in the lemon juice and fish sauce,
add the sugar, and stir-fry until sizzling.

Remove the wok from the heat. Remove the steak
from the liquid with a slotted spoon and toss together
with the papayas, cucumber, bean sprouts, and lettuce.

Drizzle the liquid from the wok over the salad
ingredients as a dressing and serve hot with a bowl
of chili sauce, if desired.

For Thai chicken salad with mango & cashew nuts,
cut 1 lb boneless, skinless chicken breasts into strips
and cook with the garlic and chilies as above. Add
½ cup lemon juice, 1 tablespoon fish sauce, and
2 teaspoons superfine sugar. Chop 2 ripe mangoes.
Toss the meat with the mangoes, cucumber matchsticks,
and bean sprouts. Serve hot on a bed of fresh cilantro
leaves instead of lettuce, drizzled with the liquid from the
wok and sprinkled with ½ cup toasted and roughly
chopped cashew nuts.

mushrooms on toast

Serves **4**
Preparation time **5 minutes**
Cooking time **20 minutes**

8 large **flat mushrooms**
2 **garlic cloves**, crushed
½ cup **extra virgin olive oil**
2 teaspoons chopped **thyme**
finely grated rind and juice of
　1 lemon
2 tablespoons chopped
　parsley
4 slices of **buttered toast**
salt and **black pepper**

To serve
arugula
Parmesan cheese shavings

Place the mushrooms, stalk sides up, in a large roasting pan and season with salt and black pepper. Put the garlic, oil, and thyme in a bowl. Add the lemon rind, reserving some for a garnish, then mix together. Spoon half of the sauce over the mushrooms.

Roast the mushrooms in a preheated oven, 425°F, for 20 minutes, until tender. Sprinkle with the parsley and drizzle over the lemon juice.

Arrange the mushrooms on the buttered toast, drizzle over the remaining oil mixture, and serve topped with some arugula, the remaining lemon rind and some Parmesan.

For oven-roasted garlic tomatoes on ciabatta, halve 12 large, ripe plum tomatoes lengthwise. Roast them in a preheated oven, 425°F, for 20 minutes with 2 crushed garlic cloves, ½ cup olive oil, and 2 tablespoons chopped thyme, but omit the lemon juice and rind. Cut a ciabatta loaf in half lengthwise and then widthwise and rub with a cut garlic clove. Drizzle with 2 tablespoons olive oil, then bake with the tomatoes for the final 10 minutes of cooking. Serve the roasted tomatoes on top of the bread, with Parmesan shavings sprinkled over and drizzled with a little balsamic vinegar.

baked tortillas with hummus

Serves **4**
Preparation time **5 minutes**
Cooking time **10–12 minutes**

4 small wheat **tortillas**
1 tablespoon **olive oil**

Hummus
13½ oz can **chickpeas**,
    drained and rinsed
1 **garlic clove**, chopped
¼ –⅓ cup **plain yogurt**
2 tablespoons **lemon juice**
1 tablespoon fresh **cilantro
    leaves**, chopped
salt and **black pepper**
paprika, to sprinkle

To serve
lemon wedges
olives

Cut each tortilla into 8 triangles, put on a baking sheet, and brush with a little oil. Cook in a preheated oven, 400°F, for 10–12 minutes, until golden and crisp. Remove from the oven.

Meanwhile, put the chickpeas, garlic, yogurt, and lemon juice in a bowl and mix really well until smooth and mushy. Sprinkle with salt and black pepper, stir in the cilantro, and sprinkle with paprika. Serve with the warm tortillas, lemon wedges, and olives.

For spicy tortillas with sundried tomato & chili hummus, prepare 4 tortillas as above and brush them with oil. Before baking sprinkle over a little Cajun seasoning. Make a smooth hummus by mixing together 13½ oz can chickpeas, 1 garlic clove, ¼–⅓ cup yogurt, 2 tablespoons lemon juice, and fresh cilantro leaves in a food processor with 3 sundried tomatoes, 1 teaspoon chopped red chili, and 2 tablespoons tahini paste. Blend well to form a smooth paste, adding 2–3 tablespoons water, if necessary. Season to taste with salt and black pepper and serve in a bowl with the warm tortillas.

french fries

Serves 4–6
Preparation time **15 minutes**,
  plus soaking
Cooking time **30 minutes**

2 lb **floury potatoes**
vegetable oil, for deep-frying
salt, to sprinkle

Peel the potatoes and cut them into ¾ inch slices, then again into batons for chunky fries. For thinner fries, cut them into slender batons, not much thicker than matchsticks.

Soak the fries in cold water for about 30 minutes to remove any excess starch and stop them from sticking together. Drain thoroughly and pat dry between layers of paper towels—they must be totally dry before frying, otherwise the oil will splatter.

Put some of the fries into the deep-fat fryer basket and lower them into the preheated fryer, 320°F. (Don't cook too many at a time or they will turn soggy.) Cook for 5 minutes, or until they start to soften but not brown. Raise the basket and let the fries drain for 5 minutes. Increase the temperature to 375°F and lower the fries back into the pan. Fry for about 6–8 minutes, depending on the thickness of the fries, until golden brown.

Drain thoroughly on paper towels and sprinkle with salt.

spinach, avocado & bacon salad

Serves **4**
Preparation time **15 minutes**
Cooking time **10 minutes**

1 ripe **avocado**, halved,
   peeled and pitted
2 tablespoons **lemon juice**
1 lb **baby spinach leaves**
1 small bunch of **scallions**,
   shredded into long, thin
   strips
2 tablespoons **vegetable oil**
4 **Canadian-style bacon**
   slices, chopped
1 **garlic clove**, crushed

Dressing
3 tablespoons **balsamic
   vinegar**
1 teaspoon **light brown sugar**
1 teaspoon **Dijon mustard**
½ cup **olive oil**
1 tablespoon finely chopped
   walnuts, plus extra to
   garnish (optional)
1 tablespoon chopped
   parsley or **basil**
salt and **black pepper**

Make the dressing. Mix the vinegar, sugar, and mustard in a bowl. Add a dash of salt and black pepper, then slowly whisk in the olive oil. Stir the chopped walnuts and herbs into the dressing and add more salt and black pepper, if needed.

Chop the avocado into cubes and sprinkle with lemon juice to stop it from turning brown.

Put the spinach leaves in a bowl together with the scallion strips and avocado cubes.

Heat the oil in a skillet and fry the bacon and the garlic until crisp and brown, then drain on paper towels. Scatter over the spinach mixture.

Drizzle some of the dressing over the salad, toss gently, and serve right away, garnished with extra walnut pieces, if desired.

For warm spinach & stilton salad with walnut croutons, prepare the salad as above, but omit the bacon. Make the dressing as above and toss the salad in it to coat. Cut off the crusts from 4 slices of whole-wheat bread. Butter each slice and sprinkle over 1 tablespoon finely chopped walnuts, then tightly roll and secure with 2 toothpicks. Cut each roll in half, keeping a toothpick in each half to secure. Heat the oil in a pan and cook the crouton rolls for 1–2 minutes, until golden. Remove from the pan and take out the toothpicks. Crumble 6 oz Stilton cheese into the warm pan, removed from the heat, and let the cheese melt slightly. Toss the cheese into the salad and serve each portion with 2 rolls of walnut bread.

drop biscuits

Makes **8–10**
Preparation time **10 minutes,
plus standing**
Cooking time **20 minutes**

1 cup **self-rising flour**
1 large **egg**
⅔ cup **milk**
handful of **dried herbs**
vegetable oil, for frying

Put the flour in a bowl and make a well in the center. Break the egg into the well and add a little of the milk. Using a balloon whisk, start whisking the egg with the milk. As you do so, the flour will gradually be incorporated into the liquid, thickening it slightly.

Work in more of the flour gradually, whisking continually. As the batter thickens, gradually pour in more milk. Once all the ingredients are combined, add the chopped herbs and pour into a pitcher. Let the batter stand for about 30 minutes before use to give the starch time to swell and produce a less floury result.

Heat a large skillet or flat griddle and drizzle with a little vegetable oil. Using a spoon or ladle (depending on the size you want to make), drop a little of the batter into the pan, then add more spoonfuls, spacing them slightly apart so that they don't run into each other. Cook for about 1 minute until golden on the underside, then flip the biscuits with a spatula to cook the other side. Transfer to a plate and keep warm while you cook the remainder, adding more oil if the pan becomes too dry.

For whole-wheat blueberry biscuits, combine 1 cup whole-wheat flour (instead of self-rising flour) with 1 egg and ⅔ cup milk. Omit the dried herbs and instead add ½ cup blueberries. Stir well to mix and cook as above. Serve the warm biscuits with spoonfuls of plain yogurt and drizzled with maple syrup.

cauliflower cheese

Serves **4**
Preparation time **10 minutes**
Cooking time **15 minutes**

1 large **cauliflower**, divided
  into florets
2 tablespoons **butter**
¼ cup **all-purpose flour**
1¼ cups **milk**
1 cup shredded **cheddar
  cheese**
1 teaspoon **Dijon mustard**
1 tablespoon **fresh bread
  crumbs**
salt and **black pepper**
4 broiled **back bacon slices**,
  cut into strips, to garnish

Steam the cauliflower over a pan of lightly salted, boiling water for about 12 minutes, until tender. Drain and put in an ovenproof dish.

Meanwhile, melt the butter in a heavy saucepan, stir in the flour, and cook for 1 minute. Slowly stir in the milk, then two-thirds of the cheddar, and heat, stirring constantly, until the sauce has thickened. Season with mustard, salt, and black pepper.

Pour the sauce over the cauliflower, sprinkle with the remaining cheese, and scatter the bread crumbs over the top. Put under a medium broiler until the top is golden brown. Garnish with bacon strips.

For cauliflower cheese with bacon & seed topping, prepare and cook the cauliflower as above. Make the sauce with 1¼ cups soy milk and vegetarian cheese and adding 1 tablespoon English mustard. Broil 2 bacon slices until crisp. Chop the bacon finely and combine with 1 cup fresh whole-grain bread crumbs, 1 tablespoon pumpkin seeds, and 1 tablespoon sunflower seeds. Pour the sauce over the cauliflower and scatter over the bacon and seed topping.

herbed soda breads

Makes a 1½ lb loaf
Preparation time **10 minutes**
Cooking time **25–30 minutes**

2 cups **whole-wheat flour**,
    plus extra for dusting
2 cups **all-purpose flour**
1 teaspoon **baking soda**
1 teaspoon **salt**
4 tablespoons **butter**, chilled
    and diced, plus extra for
    greasing
1 **scallion**, finely chopped
1 tablespoon **chopped
    parsley**
1 tablespoon **chopped thyme**
1 tablespoon **chopped
    rosemary**
1 cup plus 2 tablespoons
    buttermilk, or ordinary **milk**
    soured with 1 tablespoon
    lemon juice

Sift the flours, baking soda, and salt into a bowl. Add the butter and rub in with your fingertips until the mixture resembles fine bread crumbs. Add the scallion and the herbs and mix well to combine. Make a well in the center and add the buttermilk or sour milk. Mix with a round-bladed knife to make a soft dough. Turn out onto a lightly floured work surface and knead lightly into a ball. Divide the dough between 8 greased dariole molds.

Place the dariole molds on a baking sheet, flatten the dough slightly, and dust with flour.

Bake the dough in a preheated oven, 425°F, for about 25–30 minutes, until risen, golden, and hollow sounding when tapped underneath. Transfer to a wire rack to cool. For a softer crust, wrap the hot bread in a clean dish towel to cool. Eat on the day it is made.

For date & walnut soda breads, omit the scallion and chopped herbs and add ½ cup packed light brown sugar, ⅔ cup chopped walnuts, and ¾ cup chopped, pitted dates. Bake the breads as above.

green bean sambal

Serves **4**
Preparation time **15 minutes**
Cooking time **15 minutes**

2 tablespoons **vegetable oil**
4 **shallots**, thinly sliced
2 **garlic cloves**, crushed
½ teaspoon **shrimp paste**
2¼ cups **green beans**,
    trimmed and thinly sliced on
    the diagonal
2 teaspoons **sambal oelek or
    chili paste**
1 teaspoon **brown sugar**
salt

Heat the oil in a wok, add the shallots, garlic, and shrimp paste and fry over a low heat, stirring frequently, for 5 minutes, until the shallots are softened.

Add the beans, increase the heat to moderate, and fry, stirring occasionally, for 8 minutes, until the beans are cooked but not too soft.

Stir in the sambal oelek, sugar, and a little salt and continue frying the beans for an additional 1 minute. Taste and add a little more salt if necessary. Serve the sambal hot.

For okra & chili sambal with raita, cook the shallots, garlic, and shrimp paste as above. Instead of the beans, add 8 oz okra, each diagonally sliced into 3 pieces. Add 1 small, finely sliced Thai chili with the okra and cook as above. Make a raita by mixing ¼ cup plain yogurt with 2 tablespoons chopped fresh cilantro, 1 tablespoon chopped mint, and 3 tablespoons finely chopped cucumber. Serve the sambal hot with the raita in a bowl.

pasta, rice
& noodles

tuna & pasta bake

Serves **4**
Preparation time **5 minutes**
Cooking time **15 minutes**

10 oz **pasta shells**
2 tablespoons **olive oil**
1 **onion**, finely chopped
2 **red bell peppers**, cored,
   seeded, and cubed
2 **garlic cloves**, crushed
1⅓ cups halved **cherry
   tomatoes**, about 7 oz
1 tablespoon **butter**
1 cup **fresh bread crumbs**
13 oz can **tuna**, drained and
   flaked
1 cup shredded **mozzarella
   cheese** or **Gruyère
   cheese**

Cook the pasta shells in a saucepan of lightly salted boiling water for 8–10 minutes, or according to the package instructions, until al dente.

Meanwhile, heat the oil in a large skillet. Add the onion and fry gently for 3 minutes. Add the bell peppers and garlic and carry on frying, stirring frequently, for 5 minutes. Stir in the tomatoes and fry for 1 minute, until they are soft.

Melt the butter in another pan, toss in the bread crumbs and stir until all the bread is covered in butter.

Drain the pasta, add the bell pepper-and-tomato mix, and then the tuna. Mix together, then put in an ovenproof dish.

Sprinkle the mozzarella or Gruyère and then the buttered bread crumbs over the pasta and cook under a medium broiler for 3–5 minutes, until the cheese has melted and the bread crumbs are golden.

For salmon & green bean pasta, cook 10 oz pasta as above. Cook the onion and garlic in hot oil. Add 1 cup 1-inch asparagus pieces and 1 cup trimmed and halved fine green beans to the pan with the onion and garlic instead of the bell peppers and cook for 3 minutes. Add the cherry tomatoes as above. Drain and flake 7 oz can red salmon and mix with 1 cup crème fraîche (or ½ cup whipping cream mixed with ½ cup sour cream.) Toss all the ingredients together and transfer to an ovenproof dish. Scatter over 1 cup fresh bread crumbs and 1 cup shredded cheese and cook as above.

quick pasta carbonara

Serves **4**
Preparation time **10 minutes**
Cooking time **10 minutes**

13 oz **spaghetti** or other **long thin pasta**
2 tablespoons **olive oil**
1 **onion**, finely chopped
7 oz rindless **bacon** or **pancetta**, cut into cubes
2 **garlic cloves**, finely chopped
3 **eggs**
¼ cup freshly grated **Parmesan cheese**, plus extra for garnishing
3 tablespoons chopped **parsley**, plus extra for garnishing
3 tablespoons **cream**
salt and **black pepper**

Cook the spaghetti in a saucepan of lightly salted boiling water for 8–10 minutes, or according to the package instructions, until al dente.

Meanwhile, heat the oil in a large skillet. Add the onion and fry until soft, then add the bacon or pancetta and garlic, and fry gently for 4–5 minutes.

Beat the eggs with the Parmesan, parsley, and cream. Season with salt and black pepper and mix well.

Drain the spaghetti and add it to the skillet with the onion and bacon or pancetta. Stir over a gentle heat until well mixed, then pour in the egg mixture. Stir and take the skillet off the heat. Continue mixing well for a few seconds, until the eggs are lightly cooked and creamy, then serve immediately garnished with Parmesan and parsley.

For quick zucchini pasta, use a vegetable peeler to trim and thinly slice 3 zucchini lengthwise into ribbons. Heat the oil in a large, heavy skillet or wok and cook the onions as above, add the zucchini ribbons and 2 crushed garlic cloves, and cook for 4–5 minutes. Omit the bacon or pancetta. Complete the dish as above and serve with plenty of grated pecorino or Parmesan cheese.

individual macaroni cheeses

Serves **4**
Preparation time **5 minutes**
Cooking time **20 minutes**

8 oz **macaroni**
4 **smoked Canadian-style bacon** slices, diced
1 **garlic clove**, crushed
⅔ cup **heavy cream**
⅔ cup **milk**
pinch of freshly grated **nutmeg**
1½ cups shredded **cheddar cheese** or **Gruyère cheese**
¼ cup chopped **basil**
2 **tomatoes**, sliced
salt and **black pepper**

Cook the macaroni in a pan of lightly salted boiling water for 8–10 minutes, or according to the package instructions, until al dente. Drain and place in a bowl.

Meanwhile, dry-fry the bacon in a small skillet until browned but not crisp. Add the garlic, fry for 1 minute, and then add the cream and milk and season with a little nutmeg. Bring just to boiling point.

Stir in 1 cup of the cheddar or Gruyère and all the basil, remove from the heat, and stir until the cheese melts. Season with salt and black pepper to taste and stir the sauce into the macaroni.

Spoon into individual gratin dishes, top with the sliced tomatoes and remaining cheese, and bake in a preheated oven, 450°F, for 10 minutes, until golden.

For spinach & mixed mushroom macaroni cheese, cook and drain 8 oz macaroni as above. Slice or quarter 10 oz mixed mushrooms. Heat ¼ cup olive oil in a large, heavy skillet and cook the mushrooms until golden and soft. Add 1 crushed garlic clove and cook for an additional minute. Wash and pat dry 13 oz fresh spinach and stir through the mushrooms for 1 minute, until wilted. Omit the bacon. Stir in the cream and milk as above and flavor with nutmeg and cheese, omitting the basil and tomatoes. Combine the sauce and pasta and cook as above. Serve with plenty of salt and freshly ground black pepper.

seafood spaghetti

Serves **4**

Preparation time **10 minutes**

Cooking time **10 minutes**

10 oz **spaghetti**

2 tablespoons **olive oil**

2 **garlic cloves**, crushed

4 **scallions**, chopped

13 oz package frozen **mixed seafood**, including shrimp, mussels, scallops, and squid, defrosted

7 oz peeled **jumbo shrimp**, defrosted

½ cup dry **white wine**

⅓ cup **heavy cream**

large handful of **flat-leaf parsley**, chopped

salt and **black pepper**

freshly grated or shaved **Parmesan cheese**, to serve

Cook the spaghetti in a pan of lightly salted boiling water for 8–10 minutes, or according to the package instructions, until al dente.

Meanwhile, heat the oil in a skillet, add the garlic and scallions and cook for 2 minutes. Put the defrosted shellfish in a strainer, rinse with cold water, drain well, then add to the skillet. Fry for 3–4 minutes, until the shrimp are pink and scallops just cooked.

Lift the shellfish out of the skillet with a slotted spoon and reserve. Add the wine and cream to the skillet and increase the heat to reduce the sauce.

Return the shellfish to the sauce, stir well, and simmer for 2 minutes. Add the parsley and spaghetti, season, and mix well, using 2 spoons to combine the spaghetti with the sauce. Serve with Parmesan.

linguine with vegetables

Serves **4**
Preparation time **10 minutes**
Cooking time **10 minutes**

1 **red bell pepper**, halved,
   cored and deseeded
1 **zucchini**, sliced
1 **red onion**, sliced
1 small **eggplant**, sliced into
   thin rounds
8 **asparagus** spears, trimmed
⅓ cup **olive oil**
10 oz **linguine**
3 tablespoons **frozen baby
   peas**
1 cup freshly grated
   Parmesan cheese
handful of **basil**, roughly torn
salt and **black pepper**

Heat a broiler pan. Add the red bell pepper, skin side down, and cook until the skin blisters and blackens. Cook the zucchini, onion, and eggplant slices and the asparagus for 2 minutes on each side. Alternatively, cook all the vegetables under a preheated hot broiler.

Peel the skin off the bell pepper and slice into ribbons. Place in a dish with the zucchini, onion, eggplant, and asparagus. Drizzle with ¼ cup of the oil. Keep warm in a low oven.

Meanwhile, cook the linguine in a pan of lightly salted boiling water for 8–10 minutes, or according to the package instructions, until al dente. Add the baby peas for the last minute of the cooking time.

Drain the linguine and peas, then return to the saucepan. Add the vegetables, seasoning, and Parmesan. Toss well, adding the remaining oil, if necessary. Add the basil and toss again, then serve.

For linguine in basil-flavored oil with baby peas, cook and drain 10 oz linguine. Heat 3 tablespoons olive oil in a pan and cook 1 thinly sliced garlic clove for 1 minute. Put ⅔ cup olive oil in a food processor or blender with a large bunch of basil leaves and the garlic-infused oil. Process to form a green oil. Cook 1¼ cups baby peas and combine with the linguine. Pour the flavored oil over the pasta and toss well. Serve with grated Parmesan cheese.

spicy mediterranean pasta

Serves **4**
Preparation time **10 minutes**
Cooking time **5 minutes**

1 cup pitted **black olives**
1 **red chili**, seeded and sliced
¼ cup **capers** in brine, drained
2 tablespoons **sundried tomato paste**
3 tablespoons chopped **basil**
3 tablespoons chopped **parsley** or **chervil**
4 **tomatoes**, chopped
½ cup **olive oil**
12 oz fresh **ribbon pasta** or **pasta shapes**
salt and **black pepper**
Parmesan cheese shavings, to serve

Place the olives, chili, and capers in a food processor or blender and process until finely chopped. Alternatively, finely chop them by hand. Mix with the sundried tomato paste, herbs, tomatoes, and oil, and season with salt and black pepper to taste.

Cook the pasta in plenty of lightly salted boiling water for 2–3 minutes, or according to the package instructions, until al dente. Drain and return to the saucepan.

Add the olive mixture and toss the ingredients together lightly over a low heat for 2 minutes. Serve sprinkled with Parmesan shavings.

For spicy eggplant pasta with pine nuts, cook and drain 12 oz pasta. Roughly chop 1 large eggplant and toss with ¼ cup olive oil. Roast in a preheated oven, 400°F, for 20–25 minutes, until turning golden and soft. Toss 1¼ cups pitted olives and a sliced red chili with 2 tablespoons sundried tomato paste, herbs, and tomato as above, but omitting the capers and remaining oil. Put in a pan with ¼ cup water and the eggplant and heat for 2–3 minutes. Toss with the pasta and serve in warmed bowls with lightly toasted pine nuts and Parmesan cheese scattered over and with warm crusty bread on the side.

pepperoni & wilted spinach risotto

Serves **4**

Preparation time **5 minutes**

Cooking time **25 minutes**

4 tablespoons **butter**

1 tablespoon **olive oil**

3½ oz **pepperoni**, thinly sliced

½ cup **pine nuts**

1 tablespoon **paprika**

2 **garlic cloves**, crushed

2 cups **risotto rice**

5 cups hot **chicken stock**

8 oz **baby spinach leaves**

½ cup **raisins**

salt and **black pepper**

Melt the butter with the oil in a large, heavy saucepan. Add the pepperoni and pine nuts and cook gently for about 3 minutes, or until the pine nuts are golden. Drain with a slotted spoon and set aside.

Add the paprika, garlic, and rice to the pan and stir well to coat the grains with the butter and oil. Add the hot stock, a large ladleful at a time, stirring until each addition is absorbed into the rice. Continue adding stock in this way, cooking until the rice is creamy but the grains are still firm. This should take about 20 minutes.

Return the pepperoni and pine nuts to the pan with the spinach and raisins. Cook over gentle heat, stirring the spinach into the rice until wilted. Season with salt and black pepper to taste. Cover and let the risotto rest for a few minutes before serving.

For chorizo & butternut squash risotto, heat 1 tablespoon olive oil in a pan and cook 6 oz thinly sliced chorizo sausage for 2–3 minutes, until golden. Cut 11½ oz butternut squash into small cubes, add to the pan, and cook for an additional 2 minutes. Add the rice (omit the garlic) and stir well. Gradually add 5 cups stock as above. Serve in warmed bowls.

parma ham & sweet potato risotto

Serves **4**

Preparation time **5 minutes**

Cooking time **25 minutes**

2 medium **sweet potatoes**,
  scrubbed and cut into
  ½ inch chunks

4 tablespoons **butter**

1 bunch of **scallions**, finely
  sliced

2 cups **risotto rice**

2 **bay leaves**

5 cups hot **chicken stock** or
  vegetable stock

3 tablespoons **olive oil**

3 oz **Parma ham**, torn into
  pieces

1 cup chopped **mixed fresh
  herbs**, such as parsley,
  chervil, tarragon, and chives

salt and **black pepper**

Cook the sweet potatoes in lightly salted boiling water for 2–3 minutes to soften. Drain and set aside.

Meanwhile, melt the butter in a large, heavy saucepan. Add the scallions and sauté for 1 minute. Add the rice and stir well to coat the grains with the butter.

Add the bay leaves to the rice. Add the hot stock, a large ladleful at a time, stirring until each addition is absorbed into the rice. Continue adding stock in this way, cooking until the rice is creamy but the grains are still firm. This should take about 20 minutes.

Meanwhile, heat 1 tablespoon of the oil in a skillet and cook the ham until golden. Drain and keep warm. Add the remaining oil and fry the sweet potatoes, turning frequently, for 6–8 minutes, until golden.

Add the herbs to the risotto and season with salt and black pepper to taste, then add the ham and sweet potatoes, folding in gently. Cover and let the risotto rest for a few minutes before serving.

For roasted tomato, Parma ham & brie risotto, halve 8 plum tomatoes, season, and drizzle over 3 tablespoons olive oil. Roast in a preheated oven, 400°F, for 30 minutes, until lightly charred and soft. Set aside to cool. Make up the risotto as above, stirring through the roasted tomato and 4 oz creamy brie cubes at the end of the cooking instead of the sweet potatoes. Season generously and serve in warmed bowls.

chinese fried rice

Serves **4**

Preparation time **10 minutes, plus chilling**

Cooking time **10 minutes**

2 tablespoons **vegetable oil**

2 **eggs**, beaten

1 **carrot**, finely diced

½ cup frozen **peas**

7 oz cooked, peeled **shrimp**, defrosted if frozen

2¾ cups cooked **basmati rice**

2 tablespoons **light soy sauce**

6 **scallions**, trimmed and sliced

2 teaspoons **sesame oil**

scallion curls, to garnish

Heat a wok over high heat until smoking. Add half the oil, heat again, then add the eggs and cook until a thin omelet forms. Loosen and slide out of the wok, roll up, and let cool.

Heat the remaining oil, add the carrot, and stir-fry for 2 minutes, then add the peas, shrimp, and rice and stir-fry for an additional 2 minutes.

Add the soy sauce, scallions, and sesame oil and take off the heat. Mix all together thoroughly and top with the egg rolls.

Make the scallion curls for garnishing. Cut 2 onions into 1½ inch lengths, then cut each piece into very thin strips, add to a bowl of cold water with two or three ice cubes, and let stand for 15 minutes, until curled. Drain and serve on top of the fried rice.

For mushroom & egg fried rice, quarter 7½ oz cremini or oyster mushrooms and cook in 2 tablespoons vegetable oil for 2 minutes, or until golden and soft. Add 2¾ cups cooked rice and stir-fry as above. Beat 2 eggs with ½ teaspoon five spice powder, add to the pan, and cook as above. Serve with plenty of soy sauce.

shrimp & coconut rice

Serves **4**
Preparation time **10 minutes,
  plus standing**
Cooking time **15 minutes**

¼ cup **peanut oil**
1⅓ cups **Thai fragrant rice**
1 teaspoon **cumin seeds**
1 small **cinnamon stick**
4 **lime leaves**
1⅔ cups **coconut milk**
⅔ cup **water**
1 teaspoon **salt**
2 **garlic cloves**, crushed
1 inch piece of fresh **ginger
  root**, peeled and grated
pinch of **dried red pepper
  flakes**
1 lb **jumbo shrimp**, peeled
  and deveined
2 tablespoons **Thai fish
  sauce**
1 tablespoon **lime juice**
2 tablespoons chopped fresh
  cilantro leaves
3 tablespoons chopped
  dry-roasted peanuts,
  to garnish

Heat half the oil in a saucepan and stir-fry the rice until all the grains are glossy. Add the cumin seeds, cinnamon stick, lime leaves, coconut milk, measured water, and salt. Bring to a boil and simmer gently over low heat for 10 minutes. Remove from the heat, cover, and let rest for 10 minutes.

Meanwhile, heat the remaining oil in a wok and stir-fry the garlic, ginger, and red pepper flakes for 30 seconds. Add the shrimp and stir-fry for 3–4 minutes, until pink.

Stir in the coconut rice with the fish sauce, lime juice, and cilantro. Serve scattered with the peanuts.

For coconut & soy bean rice with lime & cherry tomatoes, cook 1⅓ cups rice, adding the cumin seeds, cinnamon stick, lime leaves, coconut milk, water, and salt as above. Add ¾ cup soy beans instead of the shrimp. Roughly chop a large handful of fresh cilantro leaves and halve 10 cherry tomatoes. Stir them into the rice together with 1 tablespoon lime juice and the finely grated rind of 1 lime. Stir-fry for 3–4 minutes, until hot and cooked through, then serve immediately.

nasi goreng

Serves **4**
Preparation time **10 minutes**
Cooking time **10 minutes**

2 tablespoons **vegetable oil**
5 oz boneless, skinless
  chicken breast, finely
  chopped
2 oz cooked, peeled **shrimp**,
  defrosted if frozen
1 **garlic clove**, crushed
1 **carrot**, grated
¼ **white cabbage**, thinly sliced
1 **egg**, beaten
2 cups cold cooked **basmati
  rice**
2 tablespoons **ketchup manis**
  (sweet soy sauce)
½ teaspoon **sesame oil**
1 tablespoon **chili sauce**
1 **red chili**, seeded and cut
  into strips, to garnish

Heat the oil in a wok or large skillet, add the chicken, and stir-fry for 1 minute. Add the shrimp, garlic, carrot, and cabbage and stir-fry for 3–4 minutes.

Pour in the egg and spread it out using a wooden spoon. Cook until set, then add the rice and break up the egg, stirring it in.

Add the ketchup manis, sesame oil, and chili sauce and heat through. Serve immediately, garnished with the chili strips.

For vegetarian nasi goring, crush a garlic clove and stir-fry it in 2 tablespoons oil with 1 chopped carrot and ¼ chopped white cabbage. Omit the chicken and shrimp but add 1 finely sliced red bell pepper, 4 oz sliced shiitake mushrooms, and 2 heads finely shredded bok choy. Stir-fry for an additional 2–3 minutes, until the vegetables are soft yet still retaining their shape. Add the remaining ingredients and serve in warmed serving bowls.

vietnamese beef pho

Serves **4**
Preparation time **5 minutes**
Cooking time **15 minutes**

6¼ cups **chicken stock**
2 **lemon grass stalks**,
  bruised
small piece of fresh **ginger
  root**, sliced
2 tablespoons **light soy
  sauce**
2 tablespoons **lime juice**
2 teaspoons **brown sugar**
4 oz **flat rice noodles**
1 tablespoon **sunflower oil**
9 oz **sirloin steak**
1⅔ cups **bean sprouts**
1 **red chili**, thinly sliced
handful of **Thai basil leaves**
handful of **mint**

Place the stock, lemon grass, ginger, soy sauce, lime juice, and sugar in a large saucepan, bring to a boil, and simmer gently for 10 minutes.

Remove the lemon grass and ginger with a slotted spoon and add the noodles. Cook according to the package instructions.

Meanwhile, heat the oil in a skillet, add the steak, and cook according to taste. Trim off the fat, then cut into slices. Ladle the pho into bowls immediately, top with steak slices, bean sprouts, chili, basil, and mint.

For chicken & ginger pho, cook 6¼ cups stock as above, doubling the amount of ginger. Replace the steak with 9 oz thinly sliced chicken breast. Make carrot flowers by peeling 1 large carrot and trimming the ends. Using a citrus parer, pare the carrot 5 times, spaced apart down its length to form petals, then thinly slice and add them to the pho with 4 oz noodles and the chicken. Cook for 4–5 minutes, until the chicken is thoroughly cooked. Ladle into warmed bowls and top with the bean sprouts, chili, basil, and mint as above.

ginger rice noodles

Serves **4**
Preparation time **10 minutes**
Cooking time **5 minutes**

3½ oz **fine rice noodles**
1 cup halved **green beans**
finely grated rind and juice
of **2 limes**
1 **Thai chili**, seeded and finely
chopped
1 inch piece of fresh **ginger
root**, peeled and finely
chopped
2 teaspoons **superfine sugar**
small handful of fresh **cilantro
leaves,** chopped
⅓ cup chopped **dried
pineapple pieces**

Place the noodles in a bowl, cover with plenty of boiling water, and let stand for 4 minutes, until soft.

Meanwhile, cook the beans in boiling water for about 3 minutes, until tender. Drain.

Mix together the lime rind and juice, chili, ginger, superfine sugar, and cilantro in a small bowl.

Drain the noodles and place in a large serving bowl. Add the cooked beans, pineapple, and dressing and toss together lightly before serving.

For rice noodle & coconut salad, cook the noodles and beans as above and refresh under cold running water. Put the noodles and beans in a bowl with 1⅓ cups bean sprouts and 2 cups shredded show peas and toss well. Make the dressing as above and add ⅔ cup coconut milk. Pour the dressing over the salad and turn to coat. Serve garnished with fresh cilantro leaves.

chicken teriyaki

Serves **4**
Preparation time **5 minutes**,
  plus marinating
Cooking time **5 minutes**

4 boneless, skinless **chicken
  breasts**, about 1 lb in total,
  cut into 1 inch cubes
¼ cup **dark soy sauce**, plus
  extra to serve
¼ cup **mirin**
2 tablespoons **superfine
  sugar**
8 oz **soba noodles**
sesame oil, to serve

Place the chicken in a shallow dish. Combine the soy sauce, mirin, and sugar, add to the chicken, and toss well to coat. Set aside to marinate for 15 minutes.

Meanwhile, cook the noodles according to the package instructions, then drain, refresh in iced water, drain again, and chill.

Thread the chicken cubes onto metal skewers and barbecue or broil for 2–3 minutes on each side.

Toss the noodles with a little sesame oil and serve with the chicken and extra sesame oil and soy sauce.

For shrimp teriyaki with beans & cilantro, put 24 large, shrimp in a nonmetallic dish. Make the marinade as above and marinate the shrimp in the mixture for 15 minutes as above. Blanch 1 cup thinly sliced green beans. Toss the cooked and chilled soba noodles with the sesame oil and a large handful of fresh cilantro leaves. Thread the shrimp onto skewers and cook for 2–3 minutes on each side. Serve on a bed of green noodles.

chicken with black bean sauce

Serves **4**
Preparation time **10 minutes**
Cooking time **about
 20 minutes**

1 **egg white**
1 tablespoon **cornstarch**
2 boneless, skinless **chicken
 breasts**, about 13 oz in total,
 cut into thin strips across the
 grain
about 1¼ cups **peanut oil**
1 **green bell pepper**, cored,
 seeded, and cut lengthwise
 into thin strips
1 **green chili**, seeded and
 finely shredded
4 **garlic cloves**, cut into thin
 strips
4 **scallions**, shredded
¼ cup **black bean sauce**
1¼ cups hot **chicken stock**
salt and **black pepper**
1–2 heaped tablespoons
 canned **fermented black
 beans**, rinsed, to garnish
egg noodles, to serve

Put the egg white into a bowl with a little salt and black pepper and whisk with a fork until frothy. Sift in the cornstarch and whisk to mix, then add the chicken and stir until coated.

Heat the oil in a wok until hot but not smoking. Add about one-quarter of the chicken strips and stir to separate. Stir-fry for 30–60 seconds, until the chicken turns white on all sides. Lift out with a slotted spoon and drain on paper towels. Repeat with the remaining chicken. Carefully pour off all but about 1 tablespoon of the hot oil from the wok.

Return the wok to low heat and add the green bell pepper, chili, garlic, and about half of the scallions. Stir-fry for a few minutes, until the bell pepper begins to soften, then add the black bean sauce and stir to mix. Pour in the stock, increase the heat to high, and bring to a boil, stirring constantly.

Add the chicken to the sauce and cook over moderate to high heat, stirring frequently, for 5 minutes. Taste for seasoning. Serve hot with egg noodles, garnished with the remaining scallions and the black beans.

one pot

sausage & bean casserole

Serves **4**
Preparation time **10 minutes**
Cooking time **20 minutes**

1 tablespoon **oil**
1 **onion**, chopped
1 **garlic clove**, crushed
1 **red bell pepper**, cored,
  seeded, and chopped
8 lean **pork sausages**, about
  1 lb in total, quartered
3¼ cups canned **mixed
  beans**, drained and rinsed
1¾ cups canned **chopped
  tomatoes**
⅔ cup **vegetable stock**
2 tablespoons **tomato paste**
2 tablespoons chopped
  parsley
salt and **black pepper**

Heat the oil in a saucepan, add the onion, garlic, and red bell pepper, and fry for 2–3 minutes, until they are beginning to soften.

Add the sausages and continue to cook for 5 minutes, until browned all over.

Crush half of the beans lightly with the back of a fork and add to the pan with the remaining beans, the tomatoes, stock, and tomato paste. Season with salt and black pepper to taste. Bring to a boil and simmer for 10 minutes. Remove the pan from the heat, stir in the parsley, and serve.

For rosemary & lamb casserole, cook the onion, garlic, and red bell pepper as above. Cut 12 oz lean lamb into cubes and add to the saucepan. Cook for an additional 4–5 minutes, until golden. Add 3 tablespoons fresh rosemary leaves. Crush 1⅔ cups canned flageolet beans and add them to the pan with the same quantity of whole beans as above. Add the tomatoes, stock, and tomato paste. Season and bring to a boil and cook for 25–30 minutes, until the lamb is tender. Omit the parsley and serve ladled over creamy mashed potatoes.

pesto, pea & broccoli soup

Serves **4**
Preparation time **5 minutes**
Cooking time **25 minutes**

2 tablespoons **olive oil**
1 **onion**, finely chopped
1 baking **potato**, about 9 oz, diced
1 **garlic clove**, chopped
1 cup canned **tomatoes**
3¾ cups **vegetable stock** or **chicken stock**
2½ cups **broccoli** florets and sliced stalks
¾ cup **frozen peas**
2 teaspoons **pesto**, plus extra to garnish
salt and **black pepper**
a few **basil leaves**, to garnish
freshly grated **Parmesan cheese**, to serve

Heat the oil in a large heavy saucepan, add the onion, and fry for 5 minutes, until lightly browned. Add the potato and garlic and fry for an additional 5 minutes, stirring, until softened.

Add the tomatoes and stock, and season with salt and black pepper, then bring to a boil. Cover the pan and simmer for 10 minutes, until reduced and thickened. Add the broccoli, peas, and pesto and simmer for 3–4 minutes, until the broccoli is just tender.

Garnish the soup with a little extra pesto and the basil and serve with Parmesan.

For pasta & bean soup with pesto, cook the onion and garlic as above for 3–4 minutes, add the tomatoes, stock, and 4 oz fusilli pasta, but omit the potato, broccoli, and peas. Rinse and drain 1⅔ cups canned mixed beans and add them to the pan with 2 teaspoons pesto. Cover and simmer for 10 minutes, until the pasta is tender. Season with salt and black pepper to taste. Ladle into warmed serving bowls, scatter over a few basil leaves, and serve sprinkled with grated Parmesan cheese.

thai chicken curry

Serves **4**
Preparation time **10 minutes**
Cooking time **20 minutes**

1 tablespoon **sunflower oil**
1 **lemon grass stalk**, cut into
   4 pieces
2 **kaffir lime leaves**, halved
1–2 **red chilies**, seeded, if
   desired, then finely chopped
1 inch piece of fresh **ginger
   root**, peeled and grated
1 **onion**, finely chopped
1 **garlic clove**, crushed
1 **red bell pepper**, cored,
   seeded, and chopped
1 **green bell pepper**, cored,
   seeded, and chopped
3 boneless, skinless **chicken
   breasts**, about 1 lb in total,
   chopped
1⅔ cups **coconut milk**
⅔ cup **chicken stock**
2 tablespoons chopped fresh
   cilantro leaves
salt and **black pepper**
basmati rice, to serve

Heat the oil in a saucepan, add the lemon grass, lime leaves, chili, ginger, onion, and garlic and fry for 2 minutes. Add the red and green bell peppers and chopped chicken and fry for 5 minutes.

Pour in the coconut milk and the stock and bring to a boil, then reduce the heat and simmer for 10 minutes, or until the chicken is cooked through.

Stir in the cilantro leaves and season with salt and black pepper to taste. Serve with basmati rice.

For squash & bell pepper curry, cook the lemon grass, lime leaves, chili, ginger, onion, and garlic as above. Add the bell peppers to the pan. Omit the chicken and instead add 3 cups cubed butternut squash and 2 zucchini, trimmed and cut into chunks. Stir-fry for 5 minutes. Add the coconut milk and stock and cook as above, adding 4 oz fine green beans for the final 5 minutes of cooking. Stir in the cilantro and serve with sticky Thai rice.

haddock & spinach chowder

Serves **4**

Preparation time **10 minutes**

Cooking time **25 minutes**

4 tablespoons **butter**

1 tablespoon **sunflower oil**

1 large **onion**, chopped

1 large baking **potato**, diced

3¾ cups low-fat **milk**

1 **fish stock cube**

2 **bay leaves**

freshly grated **nutmeg**

13 oz **smoked haddock fillet**, halved

4 oz **baby spinach leaves**, stems removed and torn into pieces

salt and **black pepper**

4 broiled **bacon** slices, cut into strips to garnish (optional)

crusty bread, to serve

Heat the butter and oil in a large heavy saucepan, add the onion, and fry gently for 5 minutes, until softened but not browned. Add the potato and fry for an additional 5 minutes, stirring, until lightly browned.

Stir in the milk, stock cube, bay leaves, nutmeg, and black salt and pepper to taste. Add the haddock and bring to a boil, then cover the pan and simmer for 10 minutes, until the haddock is cooked and flakes easily.

Lift the haddock out of the pan onto a plate, peel off the skin, and flake the flesh into pieces, carefully removing any bones, then set aside.

Add the spinach to the pan and cook for 2–3 minutes, until tender. Return the haddock to the pan and reheat.

Garnish the soup with the bacon, if using, and serve with crusty bread.

For shrimp & corn soup, cook the onion and potato as above. Add the milk, stock cube, and seasoning but omit the haddock and spinach. Instead add 7½ oz shrimp and 1 cup canned corn kernals. Cook for 2–3 minutes, until piping hot, then stir in ⅓ cup chopped flat-leaf parsley. Garnish with bacon as above and serve with warm crusty whole-grain bread.

chicken biryani

Serves **4**

Preparation time **10 minutes**, plus marinating

Cooking time **25 minutes**

8 oz boneless, skinless **chicken thighs**, cut into bite-size pieces

1 teaspoon **turmeric**

1 teaspoon **ground cumin**

1 teaspoon **ground coriander**

1 teaspoon **chili powder**

⅓ cup **Greek yogurt**

1 tablespoon **vegetable oil**

1 **onion**, thinly sliced

2 **garlic cloves**, finely chopped

1 teaspoon grated fresh **ginger root**

2 inch piece of **cinnamon stick**

3 **cloves**

3 **cardamom pods**

1⅓ cup **basmati rice**

2½ cups **chicken stock**

3 medium **potatoes**, about 13 oz, cut into 1 inch chunks

salt and **black pepper**

cilantro sprigs, to garnish

To serve

poppadums

Indian chutneys

Put the chicken in a bowl with the turmeric, cumin, ground coriander, chili, and yogurt and mix well. (If you have more time, let the chicken marinate for longer. Just cover the bowl with plastic wrap, then place in the refrigerator.)

Heat the oil in a heavy saucepan. Add the onion, garlic, ginger, cinnamon, cloves, and cardamom and fry for 3–4 minutes.

Add the chicken mixture and cook for 2–3 minutes, stirring often. Stir in the rice and pour in the stock. Season generously with salt and black pepper and bring to a boil. Add the potatoes, cover the pan tightly, and reduce the heat. Simmer gently for 10–12 minutes.

Remove the pan from the heat and let stand, without removing the lid, for 5 minutes. Fluff up the rice with a fork, garnish with sprigs of cilantro, and serve the biryani with poppadums and Indian chutneys.

mediterranean lamb stew

Serves **4**
Preparation time **15 minutes**
Cooking time **30 minutes**

2 tablespoons **olive oil**
1 lb lean **lamb fillet**, very thinly
   sliced
1 **red onion**, chopped
1 large **eggplant**, about
   12 oz, cut into small chunks
2 **garlic cloves**, crushed
1¾ cups canned **chopped**
   tomatoes
2 tablespoons **sundried**
   tomato paste
1 teaspoon **light brown sugar**
⅔ cup **vegetable stock**
salt and **black pepper**
crusty bread, to serve

Pesto
½ bunch of **scallions**, trimmed
   and roughly chopped
2 oz **Parmesan cheese**,
   crumbled
2 teaspoons **wine vinegar**
   or fresh **lemon juice**
3 tablespoons **olive oil**

Heat 1 tablespoon of the oil in a large, flameproof casserole. Add the lamb and fry gently for 5 minutes. Remove the lamb and set aside.

Heat the remaining oil in the casserole, add the onion and eggplant, and fry for about 5 minutes, until beginning to color. Add the garlic, tomatoes, tomato paste, sugar, and stock and bring to a boil. Reduce the heat, cover the casserole and simmer gently for 5 minutes.

Return the lamb to the casserole and stir into the vegetables. Cook gently for 15 minutes. Check the seasoning.

Put the scallions, Parmesan, wine vinegar or lemon juice, and the olive oil into a blender or food processor and blend to a coarse paste. Transfer this pesto to a small bowl.

Spoon the stew into bowls and top with spoonfuls of pesto. Serve with crusty bread.

For vegetarian Mediterranean stew, trim and cut 2 large zucchini into chunks. Core and seed 2 red bell peppers. Cook the onion and eggplant as above, add the zucchini and bell peppers and cook for 5 minutes. Add the remaining ingredients (omitting the lamb) together with 18 black olives and cook for 15–20 minutes, until all the vegetables are tender. Make a pesto with a large handful of basil leaves instead of the scallions and add 1 tablespoon pine nuts to the mix while processing. Serve the hot stew with pesto spooned over.

navarin of spring vegetables

Serves **4**
Preparation time **10 minutes**
Cooking time **25 minutes**

1 ½ cups small **fava beans**, defrosted if frozen
6 oz **sugar snap peas**, trimmed
6 oz fine young trimmed **asparagus**, cut into 1 inch pieces
6 tablespoons **butter**
8 **scallions**, sliced
2 **garlic cloves**, chopped
3¾ cups **chicken stock** or **vegetable stock**
1 **thyme sprig**
15 **pearl onions**, peeled
10 **baby turnips** or 3 small **turnips**, cut into wedges
5 small **carrots**, about 8 oz
1 ½ tablespoons fresh **lemon juice**
salt and **black pepper**
chopped **chervil** or **parsley**, to garnish

Cook the fava beans (if using fresh ones), sugar snap peas, and asparagus in salted boiling water for 2–3 minutes, then plunge immediately into a bowl of ice-cold water. This is known as blanching. Drain and set aside. Pop the fava beans out of their skins.

Melt the butter in a large, flameproof casserole over a low heat, add the scallions and garlic, and cook, without coloring, for 3 minutes, until softened. Add the stock and thyme and bring to a boil, then add the pearl onions. Cover the casserole and simmer for 5 minutes.

Add the turnips, bring back to a boil, then reduce the heat and simmer for 6–8 minutes. Add the carrots and cook for 5–6 minutes. Season with salt, black pepper, and lemon juice. Add the beans, peas, and asparagus and heat through. Serve garnished with the chopped herbs.

For navarin of lamb, blanch the beans, peas, and asparagus as above. Heat 6 tablespoons butter in a large, flameproof casserole dish and lightly fry 4 lamb chops or cutlets for 2 minutes on each side with the garlic (omit the scallions). Add the stock and thyme and bring to a boil, adding the pearl onions, scrubbed new potatoes, about 7½ oz (instead of the turnips), and the carrots. Continue to cook as above, simmering for 5 minutes, and then cooking for an additional 15 minutes. Add 4 oz trimmed baby leeks for the final 5 minutes of cooking. Serve garnished with chopped chervil.

boston baked beans

Serves **4**
Preparation time **10 minutes**
Cooking time **30 minutes**

2 tablespoons **vegetable oil**
1 large **red onion**, finely
   chopped
4 **celery stalks**, finely
   chopped
2 **garlic cloves**, crushed
1¾ cups canned **chopped
   tomatoes**
1¼ cups **vegetable stock**
2 tablespoons **dark soy
   sauce**
2 tablespoons **dark brown
   sugar**
4 teaspoons **Dijon mustard**
3¼ cups canned **mixed
   beans**, drained and rinsed
¼ cup chopped **parsley**
buttered toast, to serve

Heat the oil in a heavy saucepan. Add the onion and cook over low heat for 5 minutes, or until softened. Add the celery and garlic and continue to cook for 1–2 minutes.

Add the tomatoes, stock, and soy sauce and bring to a boil, then reduce the heat to a fast simmer and cook for about 15 minutes, or until the sauce begins to thicken.

Add the sugar, mustard, and mixed beans and cook for an additional 5 minutes, or until the beans are heated through. Stir in the chopped parsley and serve on toast.

For baked beans with bacon & grilled cheese, cook the onion, celery, and garlic as above together with 4 oz chunky bacon pieces for 5 minutes. Add the tomatoes. Omit the stock and soy sauce and instead add ⅓ cup tomato paste and ¼ cup water. Cook as above. Add the sugar, mustard, and beans and cook as above. Spoon onto slices of toast. Sprinkle ¼ cup shredded cheddar cheese over each portion and cook under a hot broiler for 2–3 minutes, until melted and golden. Serve immediately.

chicken & lemon paella

Serves **4**
Preparation time **10 minutes**
Cooking time **30–40 minutes**

2 tablespoons **olive oil**
1 lb boneless, skinless
 chicken thighs, diced
2 **onions**, sliced
3 **garlic cloves**, crushed
1 **red bell pepper**, cored,
 seeded, and roughly
 chopped
1 cup **instant long-grain rice**
¼ cup **dry sherry**
450 ml (¾ pint) **chicken stock**
1⅓ cups **frozen peas**
grated rind and juice of
 1 lemon
salt and **black pepper**
thyme sprigs, to garnish
lemon wedges, to serve

Heat 1 teaspoon of the oil in a skillet over medium heat and cook the chicken for 4–6 minutes, or until golden. Remove from the skillet and add the remaining oil. Add the onion and cook over medium heat for 10 minutes, until soft. Add the garlic and red bell pepper and cook for 3 minutes.

Stir in the rice and pour in the sherry and stock. Return the chicken to the skillet. Turn the heat to low and cook for 10–15 minutes.

Add the peas and cook for an additional 2–3 minutes, or until the liquid has evaporated. Stir in the lemon rind and juice, then season with salt and black pepper to taste. Serve garnished with thyme sprigs and accompanied by lemon wedges.

For chorizo, shrimp & chicken paella, cook the chicken as above. With the chicken in the pan, add the onions, garlic, and red bell pepper together with 6 oz thinly sliced chorizo sausage. Cook as above. Stir in the rice, sherry, and stock, omitting the peas, and cook for 10–15 minutes. Stir in the lemon rind and juice with 4 oz shrimp and cook for an additional 2–3 minutes, until the shrimp are piping hot. Add ⅓ cup chopped parsley and season to taste. Serve piping hot.

vegetable curry

Serves **4**
Preparation time **10 minutes**
Cooking time **20–25 minutes**

1 tablespoon **olive oil**
1 **onion**, chopped
1 **garlic clove**, crushed
2 tablespoons **medium curry paste**
3 lb prepared **mixed vegetables**, such as zucchini, bell peppers, squash, mushrooms, and green beans
1 cup canned **chopped tomatoes**
1⅔ cups **coconut milk**
2 tablespoons chopped fresh **cilantro leaves**
rice, to serve

Heat the oil in a large saucepan, add the onion and garlic, and fry for 2 minutes. Stir in the curry paste and fry for an additional 1 minute.

Add the vegetables and fry for 2–3 minutes, stirring occasionally, then add the tomatoes and coconut milk. Stir well and bring to a boil, then lower the heat and simmer for 12–15 minutes, until all the vegetables are cooked. Stir in the cilantro and serve with rice.

For mango & chicken curry, cut 1 lb chicken fillet into cubes. Heat the oil and cook the onion, garlic, and chicken for 5 minutes, adding the curry paste for the final minute. Remove the pits from 2 mangoes and cut the flesh into cubes. Add the mango to the pan and stir-fry for 1 minute. Add the tomatoes and coconut milk, cover, and simmer for 12–15 minutes, until the chicken is cooked. Stir in the fresh cilantro leaves and serve with rice.

meaty treats

rolled stuffed chicken breasts

Serves **4**
Preparation time **10 minutes**
Cooking time **20 minutes**

4 boneless, skinless **chicken breasts**, about 5 oz each
4 slices of **Parma ham**
4 thin slices of **buffalo mozzarella cheese**
4 **asparagus** tips, plus extra to serve
⅔ cup **all-purpose flour**
1 tablespoon **olive oil**
4 tablespoons **butter**
¼ cup dry **white wine**
⅓ cup **chicken stock**
7 oz **baby leaf spinach**
7 oz chilled package **sun-blush tomatoes** or **sundried tomatoes** in oil, drained
salt and **black pepper**

Place each chicken breast between 2 sheets of wax paper and flatten to about 2½ times its original size by pounding with a rolling pin.

Season the chicken with salt and black pepper, place a slice of Parma ham, a slice of mozzarella, and an asparagus tip on top, and tightly roll up the chicken breasts. Tie with a piece of kitchen twine or spear with wooden toothpicks.

Season the flour with salt and black pepper. Dip the prepared chicken rolls into the flour to coat evenly.

Heat the oil and half of the butter in a skillet, add the chicken rolls, and sauté over low heat for 15 minutes, or until golden all over and cooked through, turning frequently to brown the chicken evenly.

Remove the chicken, place in a warmed serving dish, and keep warm. Pour the wine and stock into the skillet, bring to a boil, and simmer for 3 minutes.

Remove the twine or toothpicks just before serving the chicken. Add the remaining butter to the skillet, mix quickly with a small whisk to emulsify the sauce, add the spinach and tomatoes, and cook for 2 minutes, until the spinach has just wilted. Spoon onto plates, slice the chicken, and arrange in a line down the center.

For cheese & tomato-stuffed chicken, prepare the chicken breasts as above. Spread each with 2 oz soft goat cheese and top with 4 basil leaves and 3 sun-blushed or sundried tomatoes. Roll up tightly and secure with kitchen twine or toothpicks as above. Continue to cook as above. Serve with fine green beans tossed with a little lemon butter.

kashmiri lamb chops

Serves **4**
Preparation time **10 minutes**,
  plus marinating
Cooking time **8–12 minutes**

1 ¼ cups **plain yogurt**
1 teaspoon **chili powder**
2 teaspoons grated fresh
  ginger root
2 **garlic cloves**, crushed
2 tablespoons chopped **fresh
  cilantro**
1 tablespoon **sunflower oil**,
  plus extra for oiling
8 **lamb loin chops**
salt and **black pepper**

To serve
pilaf rice
**cherry tomato, onion, and
  cilantro salad**

Mix together the yogurt, chili powder, ginger, garlic, cilantro, and oil in a large bowl and season with salt and black pepper.

Add the chops to this mixture and coat them thoroughly. Cover and marinate for at least 3 hours (ideally 10 hours) in the refrigerator, if time allows.

Place the chops on a lightly oiled broiler pan. Cook under a preheated hot broiler for 4–6 minutes on each side, or until tender. Serve with pilaf rice and a cherry tomato, onion, and cilantro salad.

For lamb & apricot kebabs, cut 12 oz lamb fillet into cubes. Prepare the marinade as above. Coat the lamb thoroughly in the marinade and marinate as above. Thread the lamb onto skewers, alternating the meat with red onion wedges and dried apricots. Cook the skewers on the barbecue or griddle or under the broiler for 4–6 minutes on each side, until cooked through. Serve with brown rice.

spicy hamburgers

Serves **4**
Preparation time **10 minutes**
Cooking time **6–14 minutes**

1 lb 3 oz lean **ground beef**
2 **garlic cloves**, crushed
1 **red onion**, finely chopped
1 **hot red chili**, finely chopped
1 bunch of **parsley**, chopped
1 tablespoon **Worcestershire sauce**
1 **egg**, beaten
4 **buns**, such as whole-wheat or whole-grain, split
hot salad greens, such as mizuna or arugula
1 **beefsteak tomato**, sliced
salt and **black pepper**
snipped **chives**, to garnish

To serve
burger relish
grilled new potatoes

Put the ground beef, garlic, red onion, chili, and parsley in a large bowl. Add the Worcestershire sauce, beaten egg, and a little salt and black pepper and mix well.

Heat a griddle or ridged grill pan. Using your hands, divide the ground meat mixture into 4 and shape into burgers. Cook the burgers in the griddle for 3 minutes on each side for rare, 5 minutes for medium, or 7 minutes for well done.

Place the bun halves under a preheated hot broiler and toast on one side. Fill each bun with some hot salad greens, some tomato slices, and a grilled burger, garnish with snipped chives and serve with your favorite relish and new potatoes.

For pork & apple burgers, mix 1 lb 3 oz ground pork with the garlic, red onion, chili, and parsley in a large bowl as above. Peel, core, and finely chop 1 small red apple and add to the bowl. Omit the Worcestershire sauce, but add the egg to the bowl and season well. Shape the mixture into burgers and cook. Shred Wensleydale cheese or another hard cheese of your choice over the top while the burgers are warm and serve in the halved buns as above.

sausages & mustard mash

Serves **4**
Preparation time **5 minutes**
Cooking time **25 minutes**

8 **sausages**
2 **onions**, cut into wedges
2 **apples**, cored and cut into
wedges
1 tablespoon **all-purpose
flour**
1 cup **chicken stock**

Mustard mash
2 lb **potatoes**, quartered and
scrubbed
6 tablespoons **butter**
1–2 tablespoons whole-grain
mustard
1 **garlic clove**, crushed
salt and **black pepper**
1 large bunch of **parsley**,
chopped
dash of **olive oil**

Put the potatoes into a large saucepan of cold water,
bring to a boil, and simmer for 15 minutes, until tender.

Meanwhile, fry the sausages over medium heat for
10 minutes, turning to get an even color. Add the onion
and apple wedges and cook with the sausages for
6–7 minutes.

Drain the potatoes well. When they are cool enough
to touch, peel them, then mash well so they are nice
and creamy.

Add the butter, mustard, garlic, and a good sprinkling
of salt and black pepper to the potatoes, and carry on
mashing. Taste and add more mustard, if you want.
Finally, stir in the parsley and olive oil.

Transfer the sausages, onion, and apple to a serving
plate. Pour off the excess fat from the pan to leave
about 1 tablespoon, then mix in the flour. Gradually stir
in the stock, bring to a boil, and stir until thickened.
Season and strain into a pitcher.

Pile the mash up on a plate and add the sausages and
onion wedges on top. Spoon over the gravy and serve.

For cheesy mash potatoes with stir-fried leeks,
finely slice 2 medium leeks. Heat 4 tablespoons butter
in a pan and cook the leeks for 5–6 minutes over gentle
heat, until softened and beginning to turn golden in
places. Set aside. Cook and mash the potatoes as
above, but omit the garlic and instead add 1 cup
shredded grated cheddar cheese. Stir well to mix and
make a creamy mash. Fold through the stir-fried leeks
and season well. Serve with the sausages as above.

chargrilled chicken with salsa

Serves **4**
Preparation time **10 minutes**,
  plus marinating
Cooking time **18 minutes**

2 tablespoons **dark soy
  sauce**
2 teaspoons **sesame oil**
1 tablespoon **olive oil**
2 teaspoons **honey**
pinch of **dried red pepper
  flakes**
4 large boneless, skinless
  chicken breasts, about
  7 oz each

Salsa
1 **red onion**, diced
1 small **garlic clove**, crushed
1 bunch of fresh **cilantro
  leaves**, roughly chopped
⅓ cup **extra virgin olive oil**
grated rind and juice of
  1 lemon
1 teaspoon **ground cumin**
salt and **black pepper**

To serve
diced **tomato**
couscous

Combine the soy sauce, sesame oil, olive oil, honey, and dried red pepper flakes in a shallow dish. Add the whole chicken breasts, cover, and let marinate for 3–4 hours in the refrigerator.

Preheat a griddle or ridged grill pan over high heat until hot, then add the chicken, reduce the heat to medium, and cook for 8 minutes on each side, until chargrilled and cooked through. Wrap in aluminum foil and let rest for 5 minutes.

Meanwhile, mix all the salsa ingredients together and season with salt and black pepper. Set aside to infuse.

Strain the marinade juices into a small saucepan and bring to a boil, then remove from the heat.

Serve the chicken with the couscous tossed with diced tomato and top with the salsa and the warm marinade.

For salmon with mango & chili salsa, prepare the marinade as above. Coat 4 salmon fillets, each about 6 oz, in the marinade and let stand at room temperature for 2 hours before grilling for 2–3 minutes on each side, until slightly blackened. Cut ½ mango into small dice. Prepare the salsa as above, but with ½ red onion and omitting the garlic. Add the mango. Finely slice a Thai chili and stir through the salsa. Serve the hot salmon with the salsa spooned over.

lamb with beet salad

Serves **4**
Preparation time **5 minutes**
Cooking time **20 minutes**

⅔ cup **French green lentils**
1 cup fine **green beans**
¼ cup **extra virgin olive oil**
2 **lamb shoulder chops** or
   lamb loins, about 10 oz
   each
¼ cup **red wine**
1 tablespoon **red wine
   vinegar**
2⅔ cups drained and diced,
   cooked beets
1 small bunch of **mint**, roughly
   chopped
salt and **black pepper**

Put the lentils into a saucepan, cover with cold water, and simmer for 20 minutes. Drain well and transfer to a bowl.

Meanwhile, cook the green beans in salted boiling water for 2–3 minutes, then plunge immediately into a bowl of ice-cold water. This is known as blanching. Drain and pat dry on paper towels.

Heat 1 tablespoon of the oil in a skillet and fry the lamb for 7 minutes, turning once. Transfer to a preheated low oven, 300°F, to rest for 5 minutes, reserving the juices in the pan.

Add the wine to the pan juices and boil until only about 1 tablespoon remains. Remove from the heat, and whisk in the vinegar and the remaining oil, and season with salt and black pepper to taste.

Combine the lentils, beans, beets, and mint in a bowl, add the dressing, and toss to coat. Serve with the lamb.

For bacon & French green lentil salad, heat 1 tablespoon olive oil in a large, heavy skillet and cook 1 large, finely chopped onion for 3–4 minutes, until softened. Add 4 oz roughly chopped bacon and cook for an additional 3–4 minutes, until golden. Add the lentils as above together with 1¼ cups chicken stock and bring to a boil. Reduce the heat, cover, and simmer for 20 minutes, until the lentils are cooked, adding more water, if necessary. Cook the green beans as above and plunge into cold water. Mix the beans with the warm lentils and serve.

steak with mozzarella

Serves **4**

Preparation time **10 minutes**

Cooking time **18–22 minutes**

2 tablespoons **vegetable oil**

4 round or sirloin **steaks**, about 8 oz each

2 tablespoons **olive oil**

1 **onion**, finely chopped

1 **garlic clove**, crushed

1 **zucchini**, diced

1 **yellow bell pepper**, cored, seeded, and diced

1 **eggplant**, diced

6 **plum tomatoes**, skinned and diced

10 **basil leaves**, chopped

4 thick slices of **mozzarella cheese**

salt and **black pepper**

basil or **flat-leaf parsley sprigs**, to garnish

Heat the vegetable oil in a shallow pan over medium heat. Add the steaks and cook for about 2–4 minutes on each side, or according to taste. Season, remove from the pan, and keep warm.

Add the olive oil to the same pan and sauté the onion and garlic until golden and crispy. Add the zucchini, yellow bell pepper, and eggplant, and cook for a few minutes. Add the tomatoes to the pan with a little salt and black pepper, then add the basil.

Place the steaks on a baking sheet. Top each one with a quarter of the vegetables and a thick slice of mozzarella. Place in a preheated oven, 400°F, for about 5 minutes, or until the mozzarella is slightly melted. Serve garnished with a sprig of basil or parsley.

For cod steaks with cheddar cheese, sprinkle lemon juice over 4 cod loins, each about 6 oz, and season with salt and black pepper to taste. Prepare the vegetable mixture as above. Arrange the fish on a lightly greased baking sheet and spoon over the vegetable mixture. Top with thick slices of cheddar cheese. Bake as above for about 15 minutes, or until the fish is opaque and cooked through and the cheese has melted.

roast pork with fennel

Serves **4**
Preparation time **10 minutes**
Cooking time **30 minutes**

1 ¼ lb **pork tenderloin**
1 large **rosemary sprig**,
    broken into short lengths,
    plus extra sprigs to garnish
3 **garlic cloves**, peeled and
    sliced
¼ cup **olive oil**
1 large **fennel bulb**, trimmed
    and cut into wedges, central
    core removed
1 large **red onion**, cut into
    wedges
1 large **red bell pepper**,
    halved, seeded and cut into
    chunks
⅔ cup **white wine**
3 oz **mascarpone cheese**
    (optional)
salt and **black pepper**

Pierce the pork with a sharp knife and insert the pieces of rosemary and garlic evenly all over the meat. Heat half the oil in a roasting pan on the stove top, add the pork, and cook for 5 minutes, or until browned all over.

Add the fennel, onion, and red bell pepper to the roasting pan and drizzle the vegetables with the remaining oil. Season well with salt and black pepper. Roast in a preheated oven, 450°F, for 20 minutes, or until the juices run clear when the pork is pierced in the center with a knife.

Transfer the pork and vegetables to a serving plate and keep hot in the oven. Add the wine to the roasting pan and simmer on the stove top until slightly reduced. Stir in the mascarpone, if using.

Cut the pork into slices and arrange on serving plates with spoonfuls of the roasted vegetables and a spoonful or two of the sauce. Serve immediately garnished with rosemary sprigs.

For roast pork with apples & cider sauce, pierce the pork, flavor with rosemary, and fry as above. Thickly slice 6 apples with assorted color skins. Heat 4 tablespoons butter and 1 tablespoon olive oil in a large skillet and fry the onion, red bell pepper, and apples for 4–5 minutes over moderately high heat, until golden and soft. Transfer to a roasting pan, arrange the pork on top, and roast as above. Keep the meat and vegetables warm. Make the sauce as above with ⅔ cup hard cider instead of wine and reduce before stirring in the mascarpone and 1 teaspoon Dijon mustard. Season to taste and serve as above.

cashew nut chicken

Serves **4**
Preparation time **10 minutes**
Cooking time **20 minutes**

1 **onion**, roughly chopped
¼ cup **tomato paste**
⅓ cup **cashew nuts**
2 teaspoons **garam masala**
2 **garlic cloves**, crushed
1 tablespoon **lemon juice**
¼ teaspoon **turmeric**
2 teaspoons **sea salt**
1 tablespoon **plain yogurt**
2 tablespoons **vegetable oil**
3 tablespoons chopped fresh
   cilantro leaves, plus extra to
   garnish
⅓ cup chopped **dried
   apricots**
1 lb **chicken thighs**, skinned,
   boned, and cut into bite-size
   pieces
1¼ cups **chicken stock**
toasted **cashew nuts**,
   to garnish

To serve
rice
poppadums

Put the onion, tomato paste, cashew nuts, garam masala, garlic, lemon juice, turmeric, salt, and yogurt into a food processor or blender and process until fairly smooth. Set aside.

Heat the oil in a large, nonstick skillet and, when hot, pour in the spice mixture. Fry, stirring, for 2 minutes over medium heat. Add half the cilantro, the apricots, and chicken to the skillet and stir-fry for 1 minute.

Pour in the stock, cover, and simmer for 10–12 minutes, or until the chicken is cooked through and tender. Stir in the remaining cilantro and serve with rice and poppadums, garnished with toasted cashew nuts and extra cilantro.

For shrimp with cashews & snow peas, make the spice mixture as above and fry over low heat for 2 minutes. Omit the chicken and apricots, but add half the fresh cilantro as above together with 10 oz shrimp and 2¾ cups halved snow peas. Stir-fry for 1–2 minutes, then add the stock. Cover and cook as above. Garnish with the remaining cilantro and the cashew nuts and serve immediately.

kheema aloo

Serves **4**
Preparation time **10 minutes**
Cooking time **15–20 minutes**

1 tablespoon **vegetable oil**
4 **cardamom pods**
1 **cinnamon stick**
3 **cloves**
2 **onions**, finely chopped
12 oz **ground lamb**
2 teaspoons **garam masala**
2 teaspoons **chili powder**
2 **garlic cloves**, crushed
2 teaspoons grated fresh
  ginger root
2 teaspoons **salt**
2 medium **potatoes**, about
  7 oz, cut into ½ inch cubes
1 cup canned **chopped
  tomatoes**
½ cup hot **water**
¼ cup chopped fresh **cilantro
  leaves**
rice or **flatbread**, to serve

Heat the oil in a nonstick skillet and, when hot, add the cardamom, cinnamon, and cloves. Fry for 1 minute, then add the onions and fry, stirring, for 3–4 minutes.

Add the lamb to the skillet with the garam masala, chili powder, garlic, ginger, and salt. Stir well to break up the meat and fry for 5–7 minutes.

Add the potatoes, tomatoes, and the measured hot water, cover, and simmer gently for 5 minutes, or until the potatoes are tender.

Stir in the cilantro and serve with rice or flatbread.

For eggplant curry, finely chop 1 large eggplant. Cook the spices and onion as above. Omit the meat. Add 3 more tablespoons vegetable oil to the skillet, add the eggplant, and cook for an additional 5–7 minutes. Add the spices, potatoes, tomatoes, and water and simmer gently as above. Add 13 oz fresh washed spinach leaves to the skillet for the final 3 minutes of cooking. Stir in the cilantro and serve with rice or warm naan.

beef stroganoff

Serves **4**
Preparation time **10 minutes**
Cooking time **15 minutes**

4 tablespoons **butter**
3 **onions**, finely chopped
3½ cups thinly sliced **white mushrooms**
1 **green bell pepper**, seeded and cut into fine strips
1 lb **beef tenderloin** or good **round steak**, cut into strips 2 inches long and ¼ inch thick
⅔ cup **sour cream**
salt and **black pepper**
1 teaspoon chopped **parsley**, to garnish

Melt half the butter in a large, deep skillet and fry the onions until pale golden. Add the mushrooms and green bell pepper to the skillet and cook for 5 minutes. Remove the onions, mushrooms, and green bell pepper from the skillet.

Melt the remaining butter and heat, then fry the steak strips for about 4 minutes, turning so they are all cooked evenly.

Return the onions, mushrooms, and bell peppers to the skillet and season well, then stir in the sour cream and blend well. Heat until piping hot, but do not let boil. Garnish with chopped parsley.

For mixed mushroom stroganoff, cook the onions in the butter as above. Halve or quarter 1½ lb assorted mushrooms, such as cremini, common, oyster, shiitake, or wild, or leave them whole if small, and add to the pan. Omit the green bell pepper and cook the mushrooms over high heat for 4 minutes. Add 1 tablespoon brandy to the skillet and stir to mix. Add 1¼ cups sour cream mixed with 1 tablespoon whole-grain mustard to the skillet and heat for 1 minute, stirring continually, until piping hot. Garnish with parsley and serve with rice.

sweet & sour pork

Serves **4**
Preparation time **10 minutes**
Cooking time **10 minutes**

2 tablespoons **vegetable oil**
10 oz **pork tenderloin**, thinly
  sliced
1 large **onion**, sliced
2 **tomatoes**, quartered
½ **cucumber**, cut into chunks
¾ cup drained **pineapple
  chunks**
1 **green bell pepper** or **red
  bell pepper**, cored, seeded,
  and thinly sliced
1¼ cups store-bought **sweet
  and sour sauce**
rice or **noodles**, to serve

Heat the oil in a wok or large skillet until really hot. Add the pork and onion and stir-fry over high heat for about 2–3 minutes, until just beginning to brown.

Add the tomatoes, cucumber, pineapple, and bell pepper and stir-fry for another 3 minutes.

Add the sweet and sour sauce and mix well, stirring constantly for 1 minute. Serve with rice or noodles.

For sweet & sour pork balls, mix 8 oz finely ground pork in a bowl with 1 teaspoon five spice powder and 2 teaspoons finely grated, fresh ginger and mix well. Shape into 16 walnut-size balls and chill for 10 minutes. Make up a batter with ⅔ cup all-purpose flour, ¼ cup cornstarch, 2 teaspoons baking powder, and a pinch of salt. Whisk with ¾ cup water and 1 tablespoon sesame oil until a smooth batter is formed. Fill a medium pan halfway with vegetable oil and heat until a cube of bread turns golden in 30 seconds. Dip each of the pork balls into the batter, quickly drop them into the hot oil, and cook for 2–3 minutes, until golden and crisp. Remove from the oil with a slotted spoon and drain on paper towels. Stir-fry the other ingredients as above (except the pork tenderloin), adding the fried pork balls at the end.

chicken with chili jam

Serves **4**
Preparation time **5 minutes**
Cooking time **25 minutes**

4 boneless, skinless **chicken
    breasts**, about 4 oz each
fresh **cilantro leaves**,
    to garnish
rice noodles, to serve

Chili jam
¾ cup cored, seeded, and
    chopped mild **red chilies**
1 **garlic clove**, crushed
1 **onion**, chopped
2 inch piece of fresh **ginger
    root**, peeled and chopped
½ cup **white vinegar**
4 cups **sugar**

Place all the chili jam ingredients in a small saucepan
and bring to a boil, then reduce the heat and simmer
for 15 minutes. The mixture should be thick, sticky, and
jamlike, and will become more so as it cools.

Meanwhile, heat a griddle or ridged grill pan. Place
the chicken breasts in the griddle, skin side down, and
cook for 10 minutes. Turn the chicken over and cook
for an additional 10 minutes.

Serve the chicken on a bed of noodles, with some
of the chili jam poured over the top, and garnish
with cilantro. Store any remaining chili jam in the
refrigerator, covered, for up to 1 week, and use it as
an accompaniment to spice up other grilled meats.

For chili jam & warm chicken sandwich, lightly toast
4 slices of whole-wheat or whole-grain bread. Spread
a generous spoonful of chili jam over 2 slices and
1 tablespoon mayonnaise over the other slices. Grill
the chicken breast as above and cut into thin slices.
Pile the chicken slices on the chili jam and add plenty
of fresh cilantro leaves. Top with the mayonnaise-
covered slices, sandwich together, and cut into
triangles. Serve warm.

tangerine beef

Serves **4**
Preparation time **about
    15 minutes**, plus freezing,
    soaking and marinating
Cooking time **15 minutes**

1 piece of **round steak**,
    weighing about 1 lb
3 tablespoons **peanut oil**
4 **shallots**, cut lengthwise
    into chunks
1 cup **beef stock**
2 tablespoons **soy sauce**
2 tablespoons **Chinese rice
    wine** or **dry sherry**
3 **tangerines**, peeled and
    segmented
1 **green chili**, seeded and very
    finely chopped
1–2 teaspoons **sugar**
salt and **black pepper**
½ bunch of **fresh cilantro**,
    roughly chopped, to garnish

Marinade
2 pieces of **dried citrus peel**
    or grated rind of **1 orange**
2 tablespoons **soy sauce**
1 tablespoon **rice wine
    vinegar**
1 tablespoon **cornstarch**
1 teaspoon **sugar**

Wrap the beef in plastic wrap and place in the freezer for 1–2 hours, until it has become quite firm. Meanwhile, if using, soak the pieces of citrus peel for the marinade in hot water for about 30 minutes, until softened, then drain and chop finely.

Remove the beef from the freezer, unwrap it, and slice it into thin strips against the grain. Put the strips in a nonmetallic dish. Whisk together all the marinade ingredients, including the grated orange rind, if using, pour over the beef, and stir to coat thoroughly. Set aside to marinate at room temperature for about 30 minutes, or until the beef is completely thawed.

Preheat a wok or large, heavy skillet. Add 1 tablespoon of the oil, swirl it around the skillet, and heat until hot. Add about half the beef and stir-fry over high heat for 3 minutes. Transfer the beef to a plate using a slotted spoon. Add 1 additional tablespoon of oil to the wok and stir-fry the remaining beef in the same way. Transfer to the plate using a slotted spoon.

Heat the remaining oil in the wok, then add the shallots, stock, soy sauce, rice wine or sherry, and any juice from the tangerines. Sprinkle in the chili, sugar to taste, and a little salt and black pepper. Bring to a boil, stirring constantly, then cook for about 5 minutes, until the liquid has reduced.

Return the beef to the pan and toss for 1–2 minutes until all the ingredients are coated with the sauce. Add about two-thirds of the tangerine segments and toss quickly to mix, then taste for seasoning. Serve hot, garnished with the remaining tangerine and cilantro.

chorizo & chickpea stew

Serves **4**
Preparation time **5 minutes**
Cooking time **25 minutes**

10 small **new potatoes**,
　about 1 lb
1 teaspoon **olive oil**
2 **red onions**, chopped
2 **red bell peppers**, cored,
　seeded, and chopped
3½ oz **chorizo sausage**, thinly
　sliced
8 **plum tomatoes**, about 1 lb,
　chopped, or 1¾ cups
　drained, canned **chopped
　tomatoes**
1¾ cups drained and rinsed,
　canned **chickpeas**
2 tablespoons chopped
　parsley, to garnish
garlic bread, to serve

Bring a saucepan of water to a boil. Add the potatoes and cook for 12–15 minutes, until tender. Drain, then slice.

Meanwhile, heat the oil in a large skillet, add the onions and red bell peppers, and cook for 3–4 minutes. Add the chorizo and cook for 2 minutes.

Add the potato slices, tomatoes, and chickpeas and bring to a boil. Reduce the heat and simmer for 10 minutes. Scatter over the parsley and serve with some hot garlic bread to mop up all the juices.

For sausage & mixed bean stew, cook the potatoes as above. Fry the onions and bell peppers in the oil, then add 4 pork sausages instead of the chorizo. Cook for 4–5 minutes. Remove the sausages from the skillet and cut each into 6 thick slices. Return to the skillet and add the potato slices and tomatoes. Instead of the chickpeas add 1⅔ cups canned mixed beans. Bring to a boil and cook as above. If you prefer a slightly hotter stew, add 1 seeded and chopped red chili to the onions and bell peppers.

beef tenderloin with roquefort

Serves **4**

Preparation time **5 minutes**

Cooking time **7–10 minutes**

1 tablespoon crushed
peppercorns

1 teaspoon **dried red pepper
flakes** (optional)

4 **tenderloin steaks**, at least
1 inch thick, about 6 oz each

3 tablespoons **vegetable oil**

2 tablespoons **creamed
horseradish**

6 oz **Roquefort cheese**,
crumbled

½ tablespoon chopped
flat-leaf parsley, plus extra
to garnish

root vegetables, to serve

Mix together the crushed peppercorns and the dried
red pepper flakes, if using, on a plate. Press one side
of each steak into the mixture to create a light crust.

Heat the oil in a large skillet until very hot, then add the
steaks, crust downward. Sear on both sides until golden
brown. Turn the steaks peppercorn crust upward.

Mix the creamed horseradish and Roquefort together
with the chopped parsley and spoon onto the top of
each steak.

Cook the steaks for an additional 2 minutes for
medium or 4–5 minutes for well-done meat. Then place
briefly under a preheated hot broiler to brown the
Roquefort crust slightly. Garnish with extra parsley and
serve immediately with root vegetables, such as sweet
potatoes and beets.

pork with apples & mash potatoes

Serves **4**

Preparation time **5 minutes**

Cooking time **23 minutes**

4 medium floury **potatoes**, diced

a handful **sage leaves**, chopped

2 tablespoons **extra virgin olive oil**

1 tablespoon **lemon juice**

1 tablespoon **honey**

1 large green **apple**, peeled, cored, and quartered

1 **leek**, sliced

4 **pork tenderloins**, about 7 oz each

4 tablespoons **butter**

2 tablespoons **milk**

1 tablespoon **Dijon mustard**

salt and **black pepper**

Cook the potatoes in lightly salted boiling water for 10 minutes, until tender.

Meanwhile, mix the sage with the oil, lemon juice, and honey and season with salt and black pepper. Mix half the flavored oil with the apple wedges and set aside. Brush the rest over the pork.

Broil the steaks under a preheated hot broiler for 3–4 minutes on each side, until browned and cooked through. Set aside and keep warm.

Drain the potatoes, mash and beat in 3 tablespoons of the butter, the milk, and mustard, and season with salt and black pepper to taste. Keep warm.

Melt the remaining butter in a skillet and quickly fry the apple wedges with the leek for 2–3 minutes, until golden and softened. Serve the pork with the mustard mash, apples, leek, and any pork juices.

For lamb with apricots & mustard mash potatoes, cook the potatoes and make the mustard mash as above. Instead of the sage, combine a handful of rosemary with the oil, lemon juice, honey, and salt and black pepper. Mix half this mixture with 1 cup halved dried apricots. Brush the remaining mixture over 4 lamb loin chops and broil as above. Stir-fry the apricot mixture in butter for 1 minute to warm through. Serve the loin chops on the mustard mash potatoes with the warm apricots spooned over and with any remaining juices from the pan.

fish &
seafood

spicy tuna fishcakes

Serves **4**
Preparation time **10 minutes**
Cooking time **20 minutes**

2 medium floury **potatoes**,
    about 8 oz, peeled and cut
    into cubes
13 oz canned **tuna**, drained
    and flaked
½ cup shredded **cheddar
    cheese**
4 **scallions**, finely chopped
1 small **garlic clove**, crushed
2 teaspoons **dried thyme**
1 small **egg**, beaten
½ teaspoon **cayenne pepper**
4 teaspoons **seasoned flour**
vegetable oil, for frying
salt and **black pepper**

to serve
lemon wedges
watercress

Cook the potatoes in lightly salted boiling water for
10 minutes, until tender. Drain, mash, and set aside to
cool down.

Beat the tuna, cheddar, scallions, garlic, thyme, and egg
into the mashed potato, add the cayenne pepper, and
season with salt and black pepper.

Divide the mixture into 8 and make into thick burgers.
Sprinkle the flour over them and fry in a shallow layer
of hot oil for 5 minutes on each side, until they are crisp
and golden. Serve with lemon wedges and watercress.

For salmon fishcakes, drain and flake 13 oz canned
salmon. Cook the potatoes as above. Mix in the
salmon together with the scallions, garlic, egg, ½ cup
shredded mozzarella cheese (instead of cheddar), and
¼ cup fresh chopped dill (instead of thyme). Cook as
above, then serve with mayonnaise mixed with finely
grated lemon rind and chopped dill.

salmon with zucchini

Serves **4**

Preparation time **5 minutes**

Cooking time **15–20 minutes**

4 **salmon fillets**, about
  5 oz each

1 tablespoon prepared
  English mustard

1 teaspoon grated fresh
  ginger root

1 teaspoon crushed **garlic**

2 teaspoons **honey**

1 tablespoon **light soy sauce**
  or **tamari**

Lime zucchini

2 medium **zucchini**, about
  1 lb, thinly sliced lengthwise

2 tablespoons **olive oil**

grated rind and juice of
  1 lime

2 tablespoons chopped **mint**

salt and **black pepper**

Place the portions of salmon fillet, skin side down, in a shallow flameproof dish. The portions should fit snugly in a single layer. Mix the mustard, ginger, garlic, honey, and soy sauce or tamari together in a bowl, then spoon this mixture evenly over the fillets. Set aside.

Heat a ridged grill pan, put the zucchini and oil into a plastic bag and toss together, lift out the zucchini strips, and fry until lightly browned on each side and tender. You may need to do this in batches. Stir the lime rind and juice, mint, and seasoning together in a bowl.

While the zucchini is cooking, heat the broiler on the hottest setting. Broil the salmon fillets for 10–15 minutes, depending on their thickness, until lightly charred on top and cooked through. Transfer to serving plates, arrange the zucchini strips around them, and drizzle with the lime dressing. Serve hot.

For easy salmon en papillote, make the mustard topping and add to 4 salmon fillets as above. Slice 1 medium zucchini and combine with 1 cup asparagus tips and 8 cherry tomatoes. Add the lime rind and juice and mint and place spoonfuls of the mixture in the centers of 4 pieces of foil. Place the mustard-crusted salmon fillets over the top. Wrap the salmon in the foil, leaving a gap for air to escape, and bake in a preheated oven, 400°F, for 20 minutes, until the fish is opaque and cooked through and the vegetables are tender. Serve immediately.

blackened cod with salsa

Serves **4**
Preparation time **15 minutes**
Cooking time **8 minutes**

1 large **orange**
1 **garlic clove**, crushed
2 large **tomatoes**, skinned,
   seeded, and diced
2 tablespoons chopped **basil**
⅓ cup chopped, pitted **black
   olives**
⅓ cup **extra virgin olive oil**
4 thick **cod fillets**, about
   6 oz each
1 tablespoon **jerk seasoning**
salt and **black pepper**
arugula leaves, to serve

Peel and segment the orange, holding it over a bowl to catch the juices. Halve the segments. Mix them with the garlic, tomatoes, basil, olives, and ¼ cup of the oil, season with salt and black pepper to taste, and set the salsa aside to steep.

Wash and pat dry the fish and pull out any small bones with a pair of tweezers. Brush with the remaining oil and coat well with the jerk seasoning.

Heat a large heavy skillet and fry the cod fillets, skin side down, for 5 minutes. Turn them over and cook for an additional 3 minutes. Transfer to a preheated low oven, 300°F, to rest for about 5 minutes.

Serve the fish with the salsa and some arugula leaves.

For spiced cod with avocado & tomato salsa, instead of jerk seasoning, rub ½ teaspoon Cajun spice over each of 4 cod fillets. Make the salsa by chopping 1 ripe avocado and 2 large tomatoes and combining with the finely grated rind and juice of 1 lime and plenty of seasoning. Omit the orange, garlic, basil, black olives, and olive oil. Cook the cod as above and serve with the salsa spooned over.

broiled spiced cod

Serves **4**
Preparation time **10 minutes**,
   plus marinating
Cooking time **20 minutes**

4 thick **cod loin** or **halibut
   steaks**, about 6 oz each
1 **red onion**, thinly sliced
2 **garlic cloves**, crushed
2 teaspoons grated fresh
   ginger root
1 teaspoon **cumin seeds**,
   roughly crushed
1 teaspoon **ground coriander**
1 teaspoon **dried red pepper
   flakes**
½ teaspoon **turmeric**
juice of 3 **limes** or 2 **lemons**
4 tablespoons **olive oil**
salt and **black pepper**

To serve
lime or **lemon wedges**
rice

Put the fish steaks into a large, ceramic dish.

Add the onion, garlic, ginger, cumin, ground coriander,
red pepper flakes, and turmeric to a bowl. Add the lime
or lemon juice and oil, season with salt and black
pepper, and mix together.

Spoon the onion marinade over the fish, using your
hands to coat the fish thoroughly on both sides. Cover
and marinate in the refrigerator for 3–4 hours.

Preheat the broiler and line the rack with aluminum
foil. Transfer the fish, skin side down, and marinade to
the foil and then broil for 8–10 minutes, until the fish is
lightly browned and flakes easily when pressed with a
knife. Serve with lime or lemon wedges and rice.

For halibut curry, make the sauce as above and add
2 cups plain yogurt and ⅔ cup heavy cream. Cut
1½ lb halibut into bite-size chunks and marinate
in the spicy yogurt and cream mixture for 1 hour.
Transfer all the ingredients to a large pan and bring
to a steady boil. As soon as it boils, reduce the heat
to a simmer and gently stir once or twice, then simmer
for 5 minutes, adding a large handful of chopped fresh
cilantro leaves for the final 1 minute of cooking. Serve
with rice or warm naan.

fish casserole

Serves **4**
Preparation time **10 minutes**
Cooking time **15 minutes**

3 tablespoons **olive oil**
2 **red onions**, finely diced
2 **garlic cloves**, crushed
½ teaspoon **dried red pepper flakes**
7 oz **squid**, cleaned and cut into thin strips, tentacles reserved
7 oz **mussels**, scrubbed and debearded
7 oz **clams**, cleaned, or extra mussels if clams are unavailable
10 oz **jumbo shrimp** in their shells
⅔ cup **fish stock**
⅔ cup dry **white wine**
½ teaspoon **saffron**
8 **tomatoes**, skinned and seeded
1 **bay leaf**
1 teaspoon **sugar**
13 oz **red mullet** or **sea bass fillets**, cut into bite-size pieces
salt and **black pepper**
green salad, to serve

Heat the oil in a saucepan large enough to hold all the ingredients. Add the onions and garlic and sauté gently for 5 minutes. Add the dried red pepper flakes and mix well.

Add the squid, mussels, clams, and jumbo shrimp and stir well.

Add the stock, wine, saffron, tomatoes, bay leaf, and sugar and season with salt and black pepper. Cover the pan and simmer gently for 5 minutes. Discard any mussels or clams that do not open.

Add the red mullet or sea bass and simmer for an additional 5 minutes, then serve at once with a green salad.

For a creamy fish casserole, cook 2 white onions (not red ones) as above with the garlic and dried red pepper flakes and add 1 bunch of sliced scallions. Add the seafood as above, stir in the stock, wine, saffron, bay leaf, and sugar, omitting the tomatoes, and bring to a boil. Season to taste, simmer for 5 minutes to reduce the wine by half, then add 1 cup crème fraîche (or ½ cup whipping cream mixed with ½ cup sour cream) and 1¼ cups heavy cream. Continue to cook for an additional 5 minutes. Blend 1 tablespoon cornstarch with 2 tablespoons water and add to the casserole with the parsley and finely grated rind of 1 lemon. Stir well until slightly thickened. Serve with rice and a simple salad.

shrimp in spicy tomato soup

Serves **4**
Preparation time **10 minutes**
Cooking time **10–12 minutes**

2 tablespoons **olive oil**
2 **red onions**, finely chopped
3 **garlic cloves**, crushed
1 **red chili**, seeded and
  chopped
2 strips of **lemon rind**
2 large, ripe **tomatoes**
⅔ cup **fish stock**
1 lb peeled **jumbo shrimp**
salt and **black pepper**
2 tablespoons chopped mixed
  parsley and **dill**, to garnish

Heat the oil in a heavy skillet. Add the onions, garlic, chili, and lemon rind and fry over medium heat, stirring occasionally, for 1–2 minutes. Add the tomatoes and stock and bring to a boil. Lower the heat and simmer for 5 minutes.

Add the shrimp, season with salt and black pepper to taste, and cook, turning occasionally, for about 4 minutes, until the shrimp are pink. Garnish with the mixed herbs and serve immediately.

For white fish & vegetable stew, trim and roughly chop 2 large zucchini. Cook the onions, garlic, and chili as above, add the zucchini, and cook for 1–2 minutes. Add 8 oz peeled shrimp and 8 oz firm white fish, such as angler fish or cod. Stir in 20 black olives and ⅓ cup chopped parsley and cook as above. Serve with warm crusty multigrain bread.

grilled tuna salad

Serves **4**
Preparation time **10 minutes**
Cooking time **15 minutes**

10 small **new potatoes**, about
  1 lb, scrubbed
4 fresh **tuna steaks**, about
  6 oz each
3½ cups roughly chopped
  baby spinach leaves
¼ cup **olive oil**
2 tablespoons **balsamic**
  vinegar
salt and **black pepper**
grilled **lime wedges**,
  to serve

Place the new potatoes in a steamer over boiling water and cook for 15 minutes, or until tender.

Meanwhile, heat a griddle or ridged grill pan. Pat the tuna fillets dry with paper towels and cook in the pan for 3 minutes on each side for rare, 5 minutes for medium, or 8 minutes for well done.

Remove the potatoes from the steamer. Slice them in half and place in a bowl. Add the spinach, olive oil, and balsamic vinegar. Toss and season to taste. Divide the salad among 4 plates and serve with a slice of tuna arranged on the top of each, and a grilled lime wedge for squeezing.

For warm niçoise salad, cook the potatoes and tuna as above. Blanch 1 cup halved fine green beans and quickly fry 8 cherry tomatoes. Add the beans and tomatoes and 20 black olives to the halved warm potatoes and spinach leaves. Flake the tuna and add to the salad. Season well and serve.

five-spice salmon

Serves **4**
Preparation time **5 minutes**
Cooking time **12 minutes**

2 teaspoons crushed **black
peppercorns**
2 teaspoons **Chinese
five-spice powder**
1 teaspoon **salt**
large pinch of **cayenne
pepper**
4 **salmon fillets**, about 6 oz
each, skinned
3 tablespoons **sunflower oil**
5 cups sliced **choy sum** or
bok choy, about 1 lb
3 **garlic cloves**, sliced
3 tablespoons **shao hsing**
(Chinese rice wine)
or **dry sherry**
⅓ cup **vegetable stock**
2 tablespoons **light soy
sauce**
1 teaspoon **sesame oil**
rice, to serve

Combine the crushed peppercorns, five-spice powder, salt, and cayenne pepper in a small bowl. Brush the salmon with a little of the oil and dust with the spice coating. Cook the fish in a preheated skillet for 4 minutes, then turn and cook for an additional 2–3 minutes, until the fish is just cooked through. Transfer to a plate, cover with aluminum foil, and let rest for 5 minutes.

Meanwhile, heat the remaining oil in a wok, add the choy sum or bok choy, and stir-fry for 2 minutes, then add the garlic and stir-fry for an additional 1 minute. Add the shao hsing or sherry, stock, soy sauce, and sesame oil and cook for an additional 2 minutes, until the greens are tender.

Serve the salmon and greens with boiled rice.

For stir-fried spicy salmon, prepare the spice mixture as above. Cut the salmon into chunks and toss in a bowl with the spice mixture to coat. Heat 1 tablespoon oil in a skillet and cook the salmon for 3–4 minutes, being careful not to break it up too much. Remove the salmon from the skillet with a slotted spoon and keep warm. Add 2 tablespoons oil to the pan and stir-fry the bok choy with 2 cups snow peas or sugar snap peas and 1 cup thin julienne carrot strips for 2 minutes before adding the rice wine or sherry, soy sauce, stock, and sesame oil. Return the salmon to the skillet, stir carefully to combine and heat through. Serve immediately.

trout with pesto

Serves **4**
Preparation time **10 minutes**
Cooking time **10 minutes**

¼ cup **olive oil**, plus extra for
  greasing
4 **trout fillets**, about 7 oz each
large handful of **basil**, roughly
  chopped, plus extra to
  garnish
1 **garlic clove**, crushed
½ cup freshly grated
  Parmesan cheese
salt and **black pepper**
salad, to serve

Brush a baking sheet lightly with oil and place under
a preheated very hot broiler to heat up.

Put the trout fillets onto the hot sheet, sprinkle with
salt and black pepper, and place under the broiler for
8–10 minutes, until lightly browned and the fish flakes
easily when pressed with a knife.

Meanwhile, put the basil and garlic into a bowl. Work
in the oil using a handheld electric blender. Stir in the
Parmesan cheese.

Remove the fish from the broiler, transfer to serving
plates, drizzle with the pesto, sprinkle with extra basil
leaves to garnish, and serve with salad.

For orange & almond trout, put the trout fillets on an
aluminum foil-lined broiler rack as above. Mix together
the finely grated rind and juice of 1 small orange,
1 tablespoon chopped parsley, and ¼ cup olive oil.
Brush the mixture over the fillets and season with salt
and black pepper. Grill until golden and opaque, then
sprinkle with toasted slivered almonds. Serve with
fresh crusty multigrain bread and a simple salad.

cod & olive risotto

Serves **4**
Preparation time **10 minutes**
Cooking time **25 minutes**

1 lb **cod fillet**, skinned
1¼ cups **white wine**
1¼ cups hot **fish stock**
4 tablespoons **butter**
2 **onions**, chopped
2 cups **risotto rice**
½ cup drained and sliced
   sundried tomatoes in oil
¼ cup **olive oil**
2 tablespoons chopped
   oregano
12 **cherry tomatoes**, halved
½ cup freshly grated
   Parmesan cheese
⅓ cup chopped, pitted **black
   olives**
1 tablespoon **white wine
   vinegar**
salt and **black pepper**

Pat the fish dry on paper towels and cut into 4 pieces. Season with salt and black pepper. Put the wine and stock in a saucepan and bring almost to a boil. Set aside.

Melt the butter in a large, heavy saucepan and sauté the onions for 5 minutes, until softened. Add the rice and sundried tomatoes and stir well to coat the grains with the butter. Add the hot stock mixture, a large ladleful at a time, stirring until each addition is absorbed into the rice. Continue adding stock in this way, cooking until the rice is creamy but the grains are still firm. This should take about 20 minutes.

Meanwhile, heat 2 tablespoons of the oil in a large skillet and cook the fish for 3 minutes on each side, until cooked through. Remove with a spatula and keep warm.

Add the oregano and tomatoes to the pan and cook for 1 minute. Season lightly with salt and black pepper.

Stir the Parmesan into the risotto and pile onto plates. Top with the fish and tomatoes. Add the olives, the remaining oil, and the vinegar to the skillet, stirring for a few seconds, then pour over the fish to serve.

For shrimp & pea risotto, cook the onions in butter as above. Add the rice and cook, then add the stock as above. When the rice has absorbed almost all the stock and it is tender, add 8 oz shrimp, 1¼ cups frozen peas, and ⅓ cup chopped mint. Heat for 5 minutes with the final ladleful of stock. Stir in the Parmesan cheese and 1 cup crème fraîche (or ½ cup whipping cream mixed with ½ cup sour cream). Heat for a minute before serving in warmed bowls with plenty of black pepper.

swordfish with sage pangritata

Serves **4**

Preparation time **5 minutes**

Cooking time **6 minutes**

⅓ cup **extra virgin olive oil**, plus extra to serve

2 **garlic cloves**, chopped

2 tablespoons chopped **sage leaves**

2¾ cups **fresh white bread crumbs**

grated rind and juice of **1 lemon**

2 cups fine **green beans**, about 8 oz

4 **swordfish fillets**, about 7 oz each

Heat ¼ cup of the oil in a skillet and fry the garlic, sage, bread crumbs, and lemon rind, stirring constantly, for 5 minutes, until crisp and golden. Drain the pangritata thoroughly on paper towels.

Cook the beans in a pan of lightly salted boiling water for 3 minutes, until just tender. Drain well, season with salt and black pepper, and toss with a little of the lemon juice. Keep warm.

Meanwhile, brush the swordfish with the remaining oil, season with salt and black pepper, and sear in a preheated griddle or ridged grill pan for 1½ minutes on each side. Remove from the griddle, cover with aluminum foil, and rest briefly.

Transfer the swordfish to plates, drizzle with the remaining lemon juice, and top with the pangritata. Place the beans alongside and drizzle with oil.

For smoky bacon swordfish with creamy leeks, lightly fry the garlic, sage, bread crumbs, and lemon rind as above with 3 finely chopped bacon slices. When the bacon is crisp and golden remove the mixture from the pan and drain on paper towels. Instead of the green beans chop 8 oz leeks, add them to the skillet and cook for 3 minutes. Drain and toss with 1 cup crème fraîche (or ½ cup whipping cream mixed with ½ cup sour cream) mixed with ½ teaspoon Dijon mustard. Cook the swordfish as above and serve it on a bed of leeks with the bacon and sage bread crumbs scattered over the top.

tuna with sundried tomatoes

Serves **4**
Preparation time **5 minutes**
Cooking time **10–15 minutes**

3 tablespoons **olive oil**
1 **red onion**, finely chopped
2 **garlic cloves**, crushed
1 **rosemary sprig**, chopped
3 tablespoons **all-purpose flour**
4 fresh **tuna steaks**, about 6 oz each
¾ cup drained and chopped **sundried tomatoes** in oil
⅓ cup **red wine**
1 tablespoon **capers** in brine, drained
¾ cup pitted **black olives**
handful of **flat-leaf parsley**, chopped
salt and **black pepper**

To serve
lemon wedges
crusty bread

Heat 2 tablespoons of the oil in a saucepan, add the onion, garlic, and rosemary and sauté gently for 5 minutes.

Season the flour with salt and black pepper. Dip the tuna into the flour to coat evenly.

Heat the remaining oil in a skillet, add the tuna, and cook for 2–3 minutes, or until golden. Turn over and cook on the other side for an additional 1–3 minutes or longer, according to taste. Transfer to a dish lined with paper towels and keep warm in the oven.

Add the sundried tomatoes to the sautéed onions and stir well. Turn up the heat to high, add the wine, capers, olives, and parsley, and season with salt and black pepper. Simmer for 2 minutes. Serve the sauce with the tuna steaks, lemon wedges, and crusty bread.

For tuna & sundried tomato pilaf, cook the tuna steaks as above. Flake the flesh into large pieces and set aside. Cook 1 cup brown basmati rice, drain, and set aside. Cook the onion, garlic, and rosemary as above and add the chopped sundried tomatoes. Add the rice and stir-fry together. Add 1¼ cups shredded snow peas and cook for 1 minute. Add the wine, capers, olives, and parsley and return the flaked tuna to the pan. Cook for an additional 2 minutes, stirring occasionally and being careful not to break up the fish too much. Serve hot with a simple dressed green salad.

angler fish kebabs

Serves **4**
Preparation time **10 minutes**,
  plus marinating
Cooking time **8–10 minutes**

2 lb **angler fish fillet**, cut into
  1½ inch cubes
1 cup **plain yogurt**
¼ cup **lemon juice**
3 **garlic cloves**, crushed
2 teaspoons grated fresh
  ginger root
1 teaspoon **hot chili powder**
1 teaspoon **ground cumin**
1 teaspoon **ground coriander**
2 **Thai red chilies**, finely
  sliced
salt and **black pepper**

To serve
salad
naan bread

Put the angler fish into a nonmetallic bowl.

Mix together the yogurt, lemon juice, garlic, ginger, chili powder, cumin, ground coriander, and chilies in a small bowl, and season with salt and black pepper. Pour this over the fish, cover, and marinate in the refrigerator for 3–4 hours or overnight, if time allows.

Lift the fish out of the marinade and thread onto 8 flat metal skewers. Place on a broiler rack and cook under a preheated hot broiler for 8–10 minutes, turning once, until the fish is cooked through. Serve hot, with salad and naan.

For chili angler fish, potato & cilantro curry, make the marinade as above and add an additional 1 teaspoon garam masala to the spices. Halve 5 small new potatoes (about 8 oz) and cook until tender. Transfer the potatoes to a large saucepan with the fish and marinade. Add ⅔ cup fish stock, bring to a simmer, and cook for 10 minutes, or until the fish is opaque and cooked through. Stir in a large bunch of roughly chopped fresh cilantro. Serve with rice and naan.

sesame steamed shrimp

Serves **4**
Preparation time **15 minutes**
Cooking time **5 minutes**

10 oz **jumbo shrimp**, peeled,
  with tails intact, defrosted if
  frozen
2 **garlic cloves**, sliced
1 **red chili**, seeded and
  chopped
grated rind and juice of
  1 lime
1 inch piece of fresh **ginger
  root**, peeled and chopped
2 tablespoons **rice wine**
2 tablespoons **Thai fish
  sauce**
4 **savoy cabbage leaves**
1 tablespoon **sesame oil**
salt
mixed fresh herbs, such as
  cilantro, mint, and basil,
  to garnish

Rinse the shrimp with cold water, drain, and pat dry.

Mix the garlic, chili, lime rind and juice, ginger, rice wine,
and fish sauce in a bowl. Add the shrimp and toss well.
Set aside.

Blanch the cabbage leaves in lightly salted boiling
water for 30 seconds, then drain and refresh under
cold water. Pat dry.

Arrange the cabbage leaves in a bamboo steamer and
carefully spoon the shrimp and their marinade on top of
the leaves. Cover and steam for 2–3 minutes, until the
shrimp are pink.

Place the cabbage leaves and shrimp on a serving
dish. Heat the sesame oil in a small saucepan and pour
it over them, then garnish with the herbs.

For crab & shrimp parcels, mix together the garlic,
chili, lime rind and juice, ginger, rice wine, and fish
sauce. Add 1 thinly sliced lemon grass stalk. Drain 7 oz
canned crab and mix with 4 oz small cooked shrimp.
Toss the seafood with the marinade ingredients. Spoon
the mixture onto 8 cabbage leaves and roll them into
parcels, folding the sides in and over to contain the
filling. Secure with a toothpick in each. Steam as above
and serve warm with sweet chili sauce.

sea bass with spicy salsa

Serves **4**
Preparation time **15 minutes**,
    plus standing
Cooking time **6–8 minutes**

4 sea bass fillets, about
    6 oz each
2 tablespoons **olive oil**
parsley sprigs, to garnish

Spicy salsa
4 plum tomatoes, skinned,
    seeded, and roughly
    chopped
1 red chili, finely chopped
2 garlic cloves, finely
    chopped
⅓ cup finely chopped, pitted
    black olives
1 shallot, finely chopped
¼ cup **olive oil**
¼ cup **lemon juice**
salt and **black pepper**

To serve
tagliatelle
spinach salad
lemon wedges

Place all the spicy salsa ingredients in a large bowl. Mix well and set aside for at least 1 hour to let the flavors blend.

Heat a griddle or ridged grill pan, brush the sea bass fillets with oil, and fry for 3–4 minutes on each side. Serve garnished with parsley on a bed of tagliatelle with the spicy salsa, a spinach salad, and some lemon wedges.

For sea bass with lime salsa & spicy fries,
make the salsa as above but add the finely grated rind of 1 lime. Cook the sea bass fillets as above. Make spicy fries by cutting 4 large baking potatoes into thin wedges and toss in ¼ cup olive oil. Roast in a preheated oven, 400°F, for 20 minutes before sprinkling with 1 teaspoon flaky salt and 1 teaspoon Cajun spice. Toss well, return to the oven, and cook for an additional 10 minutes, until golden and crisp in places. Serve the fish with the fries and salsa on the side.

vegetables

vegetable bolognese

Serves **4**
Preparation time **10 minutes**
Cooking time **15 minutes**

½ tablespoon **vegetable oil**
1 **onion**, chopped
¾ cup drained and chopped, canned **baby carrots**
1 **leek**, sliced
2 **celery stalks**, sliced
1¾ cups canned **chopped tomatoes**
1 tablespoon **tomato paste**
1 teaspoon **cayenne pepper**
1¾ cups sliced **mushrooms**
12 oz **spaghetti**
salt and **black pepper**
basil leaves, to garnish

Heat the oil in a saucepan. Add the onion and fry over low heat for 3–5 minutes, until soft. Stir in the carrots, leek, and celery, then the tomatoes, tomato paste, cayenne pepper, and mushrooms. Add a pinch of salt and black pepper and simmer for 10 minutes.

Meanwhile, cook the spaghetti in a saucepan of lightly salted boiling water for 8–10 minutes, or according to the package instructions, until al dente. Drain the pasta and sprinkle with black pepper. To serve, mound up the spaghetti and spoon the sauce over the top. Garnish with basil leaves.

For vegetarian bolognese, peel and grate 2 large carrots. Heat the oil in a pan and fry the onion as above. Add 8 oz ground-texture vegetable soy protein (ground Quorn, available in health food stores) and the grated carrots, 1 sliced leek, and 2 chopped celery stalks. Fry for 3–4 minutes, then add the tomatoes, tomato paste, cayenne, and mushrooms. Simmer for 10 minutes as above. Ladle over the cooked and drained spaghetti and top with plenty of grated Parmesan cheese. Serve with garlic bread.

mushrooms in yorkshire pudding

Serves **4**
Preparation time **5 minutes**
Cooking time **25–30 minutes**

4 large or 13 oz smaller **open mushrooms**
2 tablespoons **butter**
⅓ cup **olive oil**
3 **garlic cloves**, sliced
2 tablespoons chopped **rosemary** or **thyme**
1 cup **all-purpose flour**
2 **eggs**
2 tablespoons **horseradish sauce**
1⅔ cups **milk**
salt and **black pepper**

Beer gravy
2 **onions**, sliced
2 teaspoons **sugar**
1 tablespoon **all-purpose flour**
1 cup **beer**
⅔ cup **vegetable stock**

Put the mushrooms, stalk side up, in a large, shallow ovenproof dish.

Melt the butter with ¼ cup of the oil in a skillet. Add the garlic and herbs and a little salt and black pepper and stir for about 30 seconds. Pour the sauce over the mushrooms and bake in a preheated oven, 400°F, for 2 minutes.

Meanwhile, put the flour in a bowl and slowly beat in the eggs, horseradish sauce, milk, and a little salt and black pepper until smooth.

Pour the batter over the mushrooms and return to the oven for 20–25 minutes, until the batter has risen and is golden.

Heat the rest of the oil in a skillet. Add the onions and sugar and fry for 10 minutes, until deep golden, stir in the flour, then pour in the beer and stock and add a sprinkling of salt and black pepper. Stir for 5 minutes.

Cut up the toad and pour the beer gravy generously over the top of each serving.

For vegetables in yorkshire pudding, trim and peel 2 large carrots and 2 large parsnips. Cut them in half lengthwise and then into 2 inch pieces. Trim 2 zucchini and cut them into 2 inch pieces. Heat the butter and oil in the skillet and cook the vegetables for 2–3 minutes over moderately high heat. Add the garlic and rosemary and cook for an additional 1 minute. Continue as above, replacing the mushrooms with the vegetables. Serve with the gravy

stuffed eggplants

Serves **4**
Preparation time **15 minutes**
Cooking time **25 minutes**

2 **eggplants**
¼ cup **olive oil**, plus extra for oiling
8 **tomatoes**, skinned and chopped
2 **garlic cloves**, crushed
4 **anchovy fillets** in oil, drained and chopped
1 tablespoon **capers**, chopped
handful of **basil**, chopped, plus extra to garnish
handful of **flat-leaf parsley**, chopped, plus extra to garnish
2 tablespoons **pine nuts**, toasted
1 cup **fresh white bread crumbs**
1 cup freshly grated **pecorino cheese**
salt and **black pepper**

Cut the eggplants in half lengthwise and scoop out the flesh without breaking the skin. Roughly chop the flesh.

Heat the oil in a skillet. Add the eggplant shells and sauté them on each side for 3–4 minutes. Place them in a lightly oiled baking dish. Add the eggplant flesh to the skillet and sauté until golden brown.

Mix the tomatoes, garlic, anchovies, capers, basil, parsley, pine nuts, bread crumbs, eggplant flesh, and half of the pecorino together and season with salt and black pepper. Spoon the mixture into the sautéed eggplant shells, piling it high. Sprinkle with the remaining cheese. Place in a preheated oven, 400°F, and cook for 20 minutes. Serve sprinkled with extra chopped herbs.

For cashew & raisin filled eggplants, prepare the eggplants as above. Fry the chopped eggplant flesh with 3 roughly chopped sundried tomatoes, ½ cup cashew nuts, ½ cup raisins, and a handful of chopped flat-leaf parsley over high heat for 3–4 minutes, or until the eggplant is golden and soft. Pile the mixture into the eggplant shells and sprinkle over ⅓ cup chopped mozzarella cheese. Bake in the oven as above for 20 minutes and serve with a simple arugula salad.

haloumi with paprika oil

Serves **4**

Preparation time **5 minutes**

Cooking time **5 minutes**

⅓ cup **extra virgin olive oil**

¼ cup **lemon juice**

½ teaspoon **smoked paprika**

8 oz **haloumi cheese**, cut into chunks

salt and **black pepper**

Combine the oil, lemon juice, and paprika in a small bowl and season the mixture with salt and black pepper.

Heat a heavy skillet until hot, then add the haloumi and toss over medium heat until golden and starting to soften. Transfer immediately to a plate, drizzle over the paprika oil, and serve with toothpicks to spike the haloumi.

For chili & tomato jam to serve with the haloumi, heat 1 tablespoon of oil in a pan and add 1 finely chopped red chili, 1 finely chopped shallot, 3 tablespoons sugar, and 4 roughly chopped tomatoes. Season well with salt and black pepper and cook over moderately high heat for 15 minutes, stirring occasionally until thick, pulpy, and soft. Remove from the heat and let cool. Serve with grilled haloumi.

mushroom & spinach lasagna

Serves **4**
Preparation time **20 minutes**
Cooking time **25–30 minutes**

6 **lasagna sheets**
3 tablespoons **olive oil**
1 lb **mixed mushrooms** such
    as shiitake, oyster, and
    cremini, sliced
2 **garlic cloves**, finely
    chopped
7 oz **mascarpone cheese**
4 cups **baby spinach leaves**
5 oz **taleggio cheese**,
    derinded and cut into cubes
salt and **black pepper**

Cook the lasagna sheets in a large saucepan of salted water, according to the package instructions, then drain.

Meanwhile, heat the oil in a large skillet and fry the mushrooms for 5 minutes. Add the garlic and mascarpone and turn up the heat. Cook for another 1 minute, until the sauce is thick. Season with salt and black pepper. Steam the spinach for 2 minutes or microwave until just wilted.

Oil an ovenproof dish about the size of 2 of the lasagna sheets and place 2 of the lasagna sheets over the bottom, slightly overlapping. Reserve one-third of the taleggio for the top, sprinkle a little over the pasta base with one-third of the mushroom sauce and one-third of the spinach leaves. Repeat with 2 more layers, topping the final layer of lasagna sheets with the remaining mushroom sauce, spinach, and taleggio.

Bake in a preheated oven, 400°F, for 15–20 minutes, until the cheese is golden and the lasagna piping hot.

For walnut, spinach & squash lasagna, prepare the lasagna and spinach as above. Heat 3 tablespoons oil in a skillet and cook 4 cups roughly chopped butternut squash. Add the garlic and mascarpone, season to taste, and add ½ teaspoon paprika. Mix in 1 cup finely chopped walnuts and cook for an additional minute. Assemble the lasagna, layering the squash sauce and spinach and topping with taleggio cheese as above. Bake in a preheated oven, 400°F, for 25 minutes, until golden.

couscous with broiled vegetables

Serves **4**
Preparation time **15 minutes**,
  plus standing
Cooking time **10 minutes**

1½ cups **couscous**
2 cups boiling **water**
2 **red bell peppers**, cored,
  seeded, and quartered
1 **orange** or **yellow bell
  pepper**, cored, seeded, and
  quartered
6 **baby zucchini**, halved
  lengthwise
2 **red onions**, cut into wedges
24 **cherry tomatoes**
2 **garlic cloves**, finely sliced
2 tablespoons **olive oil**
6 medium **asparagus**,
  trimmed
grated rind and juice of
  1 lemon
¼ cup chopped **parsley** or
  mint
salt and **black pepper**
lemon wedges, to serve

Pour the couscous into a large heatproof bowl, pour
over the measured boiling water, cover, and set aside
for 10 minutes.

Meanwhile, put the bell peppers, zucchini, onions,
tomatoes, and garlic into a broiler pan in a single layer,
drizzle over the oil, and cook under a preheated hot
broiler for 5–6 minutes, turning occasionally.

Add the asparagus to the pan and continue to broil for
2–3 minutes, until the vegetables are tender and lightly
charred. When they are cool enough to handle, remove
the skins from the bell peppers and discard.

Fork through the couscous to separate the grains. Toss
with the vegetables, lemon rind and juice, and herbs,
season with salt and black pepper to taste, and serve
immediately with lemon wedges.

For roasted vegetable couscous, prepare 1½ cups
couscous by adding 2 cups boiling chicken stock.
Roughly chop 1 lb butternut squash, trim and chop
1 zucchini, cut 6 plum tomatoes into quarters, and
halve and slice 1 fennel bulb. Toss the vegetables in
2 tablespoons oil and 2 sliced garlic cloves and roast
in a preheated oven, 400°F, for 25 minutes, until lightly
charred in places and soft. Stir 1 tablespoon honey
through the vegetables. Toss the vegetables into the
couscous with the lemon rind and parsley, season
well, and serve.

vegetable biryani

Serves **4**
Preparation time **10 minutes**
Cooking time **20 minutes**

1 ⅛ cups **long-grain rice**
2 tablespoons **olive oil**
3 **carrots**, chopped
2 medium **potatoes**, chopped
1 inch piece of fresh **ginger
  root**, peeled and grated
2 **garlic cloves**, crushed
1 ½ cups **cauliflower florets**
1 cup halved **green beans**
1 tablespoon **hot curry paste**
1 teaspoon **turmeric**
1 teaspoon **ground cinnamon**
1 cup **plain yogurt**
⅛ cup **raisins**

To serve
½ cup toasted **cashew nuts**
2 tablespoons chopped fresh
  cilantro leaves

Cook the rice according to the package instructions and drain.

Meanwhile, heat the oil in a saucepan, add the carrots, potato, ginger, and garlic, and fry for 10 minutes, until soft, adding a little water if the potatoes begin to stick.

Stir in the cauliflower, beans, curry paste, turmeric, and cinnamon and cook for 1 minute. Stir in the yogurt and raisins.

Pile the rice on top of the vegetables, cover, and cook over low heat for 10 minutes, checking it isn't sticking to the pan.

Serve the biryani sprinkled with the cashew nuts and cilantro.

For lamb biryani, prepare the rice as above. Cut 8 oz lamb sirloin chops into strips. Omitting the potatoes, cook the carrots, ginger, and garlic as above together with the lamb for 10 minutes. Add the cauliflower, beans, curry paste, and spices and 4 roughly chopped baby eggplants. Cook for 1 minute, then add the yogurt and raisins as above. Add to the rice and cook as above. Serve sprinkled with slivered almonds instead of cashew nuts and with extra yogurt, if desired.

artichoke & mozzarella pizza

Serves **4**
Preparation time **10 minutes**
Cooking time **15–20 minutes**

2 cups **self-rising flour**
3 tablespoons **oil**
1 teaspoon **salt**
2 tablespoons **sundried
  tomato paste**
½ cup **water**

Topping
1 tablespoon **sundried
  tomato paste**
2 large, mild **red chilies** or
  green chilies, halved and
  seeded
3 tablespoons chopped
  mixed fresh herbs, such as
  parsley, oregano, rosemary,
  and chives
⅛ cup drained and sliced
  sundried tomatoes in oil
5 oz **baby artichokes** in oil,
  drained
2 **plum tomatoes**, cut into
  quarters
5 oz **mozzarella cheese**,
  sliced
½ cup pitted **black olives**
salt and **black pepper**

Grease a large baking sheet. Place the flour in a bowl with the oil, salt, and sundried tomato paste. Add the measured water and mix to a soft dough, adding a little more water, if necessary.

Roll out the dough on a lightly floured surface to a round about 11 inches in diameter. Place on the prepared baking sheet and bake in a preheated oven, 450°F, for 5 minutes.

Spread the pizza crust to within ½ inch of the edge with the sundried tomato paste. Cut the chilies in half lengthwise again and scatter over the pizza with half the herbs, the sundried tomatoes, artichokes, tomatoes, mozzarella, and olives. Scatter the remaining herbs on top and season lightly with salt and black pepper.

Return the pizza to the oven and bake for 10–15 minutes, until the cheese has melted and the vegetables are beginning to color.

For egg & spinach pizza, make, roll out and bake a pizza crust as above, using 8 oz whole-wheat flour instead of self-rising flour. Spread ¼ cup pasta sauce or pizza topping sauce over the crust and scatter over 2 cups blanched and squeezed spinach. Break an egg over the spinach and scatter over 2 tablespoons pine nuts. Bake as above until the egg is set and the dough has risen.

curried tofu burgers

Serves **4**
Preparation time **15 minutes**
Cooking time **10–15 minutes**

2 tablespoons **vegetable oil**
1 large **carrot**, coarsely grated
1 small **red onion**, finely
   chopped
1 **garlic clove**, crushed
1 teaspoon **hot curry paste**
1 teaspoon **sundried tomato
   paste**
8 oz **firm tofu**, drained
½ cup **fresh whole-wheat
   bread crumbs**
3 tablespoons finely chopped
   unsalted peanuts
all-purpose flour, for dusting
salt and **black pepper**

To serve
4 **burger buns**
3 **tomatoes**, sliced
salad greens
alfalfa
ketchup or **spicy tomato
   chutney**

Heat half the oil in a large nonstick skillet and fry the carrot and onion, stirring constantly, for 3–4 minutes, or until the vegetables are softened. Add the garlic and curry and tomato pastes. Increase the heat and fry for 2 minutes, stirring constantly.

Blend the tofu, vegetables, breadcrumbs and peanuts in a food processor or blender until just combined. Transfer to a bowl, season well with salt and black pepper, and beat until the mixture starts to stick together.

Shape the mixture into 4 burgers. Heat the remaining oil in a large nonstick skillet and fry the burgers for 3–4 minutes on each side, or until golden brown. Alternatively, to broil the burgers, brush them with a little oil and cook under a preheated hot broil for about 3 minutes on each side, or until golden brown. Drain on paper towels and serve in burger buns, with sliced tomato and lettuce and garnished with alfalfa. Serve with ketchup or spicy tomato chutney.

For goat cheese & beet burgers, mix together ½ cup raw grated beet and 8 oz soft goat cheese with the grated carrot, bread crumbs, and peanuts. Mix ¼ cup chopped parsley into the mixture. Shape and cook the burgers as above and serve in the buns with some good-quality ketchup.

braised lentils with gremolata

Serves **4**
Preparation time **5 minutes**
Cooking time **25 minutes**

4 tablespoons **butter**
1 **onion**, chopped
2 **celery stalks**, sliced
2 **carrots**, sliced
1 cup rinsed **French green
    lentils**
2½ cups **vegetable stock**
1 cup dry **white wine**
2 **bay leaves**
2 tablespoons chopped
    thyme
3 tablespoons **olive oil**
4⅔ cups sliced **mushrooms**
salt and **black pepper**

Gremolata
2 tablespoons chopped
    parsley
finely grated rind of **1 lemon**
2 **garlic cloves**, chopped

Melt the butter in a saucepan and fry the onion, celery,
and carrots for 3 minutes. Add the lentils, stock, wine,
herbs, and a little salt and black pepper. Bring to a boil,
then reduce the heat and simmer gently, uncovered, for
about 20 minutes, or until the lentils are tender.

Meanwhile, mix together the ingredients for the
gremolata.

Heat the oil in a skillet. Add the mushrooms and fry for
about 2 minutes until golden. Season lightly with salt
and black pepper.

Ladle the lentils onto plates, top with the mushrooms,
and serve scattered with the gremolata.

For lentil-stuffed mushrooms with ham & red wine,
cook the onion, celery, and carrots as above. Cut
2 ham steaks, each about 4 oz, into strips and add
to the pan. Cook for 4–5 minutes before adding the
lentils, stock and 1 cup red wine. Add the herbs and
seasoning and cook as above. Heat 3 tablespoons oil
in a large skillet and cook 4 large flat mushrooms for
2–3 minutes on each side, until golden and soft. Pile
the lentil mixture into the mushrooms and serve on a
bed of salad greens and sprinkled with the gremolata.

squash with red bean sauce

Serves **4**
Preparation time **10 minutes**
Cooking time **15 minutes**

2½ cups **vegetable stock**
2 lb **mixed squash**, such as
   butternut and acorn,
   quartered and seeded
4 cups **baby spinach leaves**
rice, to serve

Sauce
¼ cup **olive oil**
4 **garlic cloves**, thinly sliced
1 **red bell pepper**, cored,
   seeded, and finely chopped
2 **tomatoes**, chopped
1⅔ cups drained and rinsed,
   canned **red kidney beans**
1−2 tablespoons **hot chili
   sauce**
small handful of fresh **cilantro
   leaves**, chopped
salt

Bring the stock to a boil in a large saucepan. Add the squash, reduce the heat, and cover. Simmer gently for about 15 minutes, or until the squash is just tender.

Meanwhile, to make the sauce, heat the oil in a skillet, add the garlic and bell pepper, and fry for 5 minutes, stirring frequently, until very soft. Add the tomatoes, red kidney beans, hot chili sauce, and a little salt and simmer for 5 minutes, until pulpy. Set aside.

Drain the squash from the stock, reserving the stock, and return the squash to the pan. Scatter over the spinach leaves, then cover and cook for about 1 minute, until the spinach has wilted in the steam.

Pile the vegetables onto servings of rice. Stir ½ cup of the reserved stock into the sauce with the cilantro. Spoon over the vegetables and serve with boiled rice.

For stuffed squash with beans & cheese, halve and seed 2 lb squash. Brush all over with olive oil and roast in a preheated oven, 400°F, for 30 minutes. Make up the sauce as above. Rinse and drain 3¼ cups canned mixed beans and add to the sauce. Pile the mixture into the roasted squash halves and top with 1 cup shredded Gruyère cheese. Return to the oven for 15 minutes, until golden and bubbling.

falafel cakes

Serves **4**
Preparation time **10 minutes**
Cooking time **10 minutes**

1¾ cups drained and rinsed,
  canned **chickpeas**
1 **onion**, roughly chopped
3 **garlic cloves**, roughly
  chopped
2 teaspoons **cumin seeds**
1 teaspoon mild **chili powder**
2 tablespoons chopped **mint**
3 tablespoons chopped fresh
  cilantro leaves, plus extra
  leaves to serve
1 cup **fresh bread crumbs**
oil, for shallow frying
salt and **black pepper**

To serve
4 **pita**
2 **Boston lettuce**, torn
  into pieces
minted cucumber and
  yogurt salad

Place the chickpeas in a food processor or blender
with the onion, garlic, spices, herbs, bread crumbs and
a little salt and black pepper. Blend briefly to make
a chunky paste.

Take large spoonfuls of the mixture and flatten into
cakes. Heat a ½ inch depth of oil in a skillet and fry
half the falafel for about 3 minutes, turning once until
crisp and golden. Drain on paper towels and keep warm
while cooking the remainder. Serve the falafel in
warmed split pita filled with torn lettuce, cilantro leaves,
and spoonfuls of minted cucumber and yogurt salad.

For lunchtime pita, make the falafel mixture as above.
Fill warm toasted pita with the mixture, thinly sliced
red onions, and plenty of fresh cilantro leaves. Make
a fresh-tasting raita by mixing ⅔ cup plain yogurt
with 1 teaspoon mint sauce and ⅛ cucumber finely
chopped. Serve the pita with the raita on the side.

sweet treats

scones with whipped cream

Makes **about 10**
Preparation time **10 minutes**
Cooking time **10 minutes**

2 cups **all-purpose flour**
1 teaspoon **cream of tartar**
½ teaspoon **baking soda**
pinch of **salt**
4 tablespoons **butter**, chilled
  and diced
2 tablespoons **superfine
  sugar**
½ cup **milk** (approximately),
  plus extra to glaze

To serve
butter or **whipped cream**
jam

Sift the flour, cream of tartar, baking soda, and salt into a mixing bowl and rub in the butter with your fingertips until the mixture resembles bread crumbs. Stir in the sugar and add enough milk to mix to a soft dough.

Turn onto a floured surface, knead lightly, and roll out to ¾ inch thick. Cut into 2 inch rounds. Place on a floured baking sheet and brush with milk.

Bake in a preheated oven, 425°F, for 10 minutes. Transfer to a wire rack to cool. Serve with butter and jam or with whipped cream and jam.

For lavender-flavored scones, place ½ cup milk in a small pan and add 2–3 lavender flowers. Bring to a boil, then immediately remove the pan from the heat and let cool. Use the milk to make the scones as above. Serve the warm scones with whipped cream and a black preserve, such as blackberry or black currant, to complement the flavor of the scones.

banana toffee pie

Serves **6**

Preparation time **15 minutes**, plus chilling

Cooking time **10 minutes**

Base

8 oz **graham crackers**

½ cup (1 stick) **butter**

Filling

½ cup (1 stick) **butter**

½ cup packed **light brown sugar**

13 oz can **condensed milk**

2 **bananas**

1 tablespoon **lemon juice**

1 cup **whipping cream**

¼ cup **chocolate shavings**

Crush the graham crackers in a clean plastic bag with a rolling pin or wine bottle.

Melt the butter in a saucepan and stir in the crumbs. Press the cookie mix evenly over the bottom and sides of a deep 8 inch round springform pan or similar. Put in the refrigerator for 1 hour.

Make the filling. Put the butter and sugar in a saucepan over low heat. Once the butter has melted, stir in the condensed milk and bring slowly to a boil. Turn down the heat and simmer for 5 minutes, stirring all the time, until the mixture turns a caramel color. Pour onto the cookie base and chill in the refrigerator for about 1 hour, until the mixture has set.

Slice the bananas and toss in the lemon juice. Keep a quarter of the bananas for the top and spread the rest over the filling.

Whip the cream until it forms soft peaks and spoon it over the top. Decorate with the rest of the banana slices and sprinkle with the chocolate shavings.

For extra-chocolate banana toffee pie, make the base with 8 oz chocolate-coated graham crackers and 8 tablespoons (1 stick) butter. Make the filling as above. Once the cream has been softly whipped, melt 2 oz dark chocolate and pour it over the cream. Use a metal spoon to swirl the chocolate carefully into the cream to marble it. Spoon the cream over the bananas and serve sprinkled with ¼ cup chocolate shavings.

cranberry sponge puddings

Serves **4**
Preparation time **10 minutes**
Cooking time **25 minutes**

finely grated rind and juice of
  1 orange
1 ½ cups **fresh** or **frozen**
  cranberries
½ cup **superfine sugar**
2 tablespoons **raspberry**
  preserve
7 tablespoons **butter**,
  softened
¾ cup **self-rising flour**
2 **eggs**
oil, for oiling
custard, to serve

Put the orange juice into a saucepan with the cranberries and 1 tablespoon of the sugar and cook over moderate heat for 5 minutes, until the cranberries are just softened. Use a slotted spoon to drain and spoon half the cranberries into 4 individual 1-cup metal pudding molds.

Add the preserve to the remaining cranberries and cook for 1 minute, until melted. Set the sauce aside.

Put the remaining sugar, butter, flour, eggs, and orange rind into a bowl or food processor and beat until smooth. Spoon the sponge mixture into the molds and level the surface. Cover loosely with pieces of oiled foil.

Cook the puddings in the top of a steamer or in a preheated oven, 350°F, for 20 minutes, until well risen. Loosen the edges with a round-bladed knife and turn out onto plates. Top with the cranberry sauce and serve with custard.

For double chocolate puddings, make the pudding mixture as above but omit the cranberry mixture. Replace the orange rind with 2½ tablespoons unsweetened cocoa. Spoon the mixture into 4 pudding molds, then press 2 squares of dark chocolate into each, making sure they are completely covered by the pudding mixture. Cook as above and serve with white chocolate sauce.

chocolate cookie cake

Makes **8 slices**

Preparation time **15 minutes**, plus cooling and chilling

10 oz **dark chocolate**, broken into pieces

2 tablespoons **milk**

½ cup (1 stick) **butter**, melted, plus extra for greasing

1½ cups lightly crushed **graham crackers**

5 oz **white chocolate disks**

5 oz **milk chocolate disks**

Grease an 7 inch round cake pan or similar. Put the dark chocolate and milk in a bowl set over a pan of simmering water, making sure the bowl does not touch the water, and let stand until the chocolate has melted, stirring occasionally. Stir in the butter. Remove the bowl from the heat and let stand until cool, but not solid.

Mix the graham cracker pieces with the white and milk chocolate disks, then stir the mixture into the melted chocolate, pour it into the pan, and squash it down gently. Put in the refrigerator for at least 3 hours, until firm, then cut into wedges.

For fruity chocolate squares, melt the chocolate in the milk as above. Chop ¼ cup candied cherries and roughly chop ¹/₃ cup dried apricots. Combine these with ¾ cup raisins and a small handful of miniature marshmallows and mix into the melted chocolate. Add the crushed graham crackers to the mixture but omit the chocolate disks. Stir well, then press into a lightly greased 8 inch square pan and chill for 1 hour. Remove from the refrigerator and turn onto a board. Cut into small squares to serve with coffee or larger pieces for an afternoon snack.

apricots with mascarpone

Serves **4**
Preparation time **5 minutes**
Cooking time **3 minutes**

2 pieces of **preserved ginger in syrup**, drained and finely chopped
2 tablespoons **ginger syrup** from the jar
8 oz **mascarpone cheese**
2 teaspoons **lemon juice**
4 tablespoons **unsalted butter**
2 tablespoons **light brown sugar**
8 **apricots** (about 13 oz), halved
3 tablespoons **amaretto liqueur** or **brandy**

Mix the preserved ginger with the ginger syrup, mascarpone, and lemon juice.

Melt the butter in a skillet and add the sugar. Cook for about 1 minute, until the sugar has dissolved. Add the apricots and fry quickly until lightly colored but still firm. Stir in the liqueur or brandy.

Spoon the mascarpone onto plates, top with the fruit and juices, and serve the dessert warm.

For pan-fried bananas with vanilla cream, beat 8 oz mascarpone with ½ teaspoon vanilla extract and 2 tablespoons milk to make a smooth cream. Transfer to a serving bowl. Melt 4 tablespoons butter in a skillet and stir in 2 tablespoons superfine sugar. Halve 4 bananas and cook in the butter as above, adding 3 tablespoons of brandy, if desired.

quick tiramisu

Serves **4–6**
Preparation time **15 minutes**,
  plus chilling

⅓ cup strong **espresso coffee**
⅓ cup packed **dark brown sugar**
¼ cup **coffee liqueur** or
  3 tablespoons **brandy**
7 **ladyfingers**, broken into
  large pieces
1½ cups **custard** or **ready-to-eat vanilla pudding**
  (about 13 oz)
8 oz **mascarpone cheese**
1 teaspoon **vanilla extract**
3 oz **dark chocolate**, finely
  chopped
unsweetened cocoa,
  for dusting

Mix the coffee with 2 tablespoons of the sugar and the liqueur or brandy in a medium bowl. Toss the ladyfingers in the mixture and turn into a serving dish, spooning over any excess liquid.

Beat together the custard, mascarpone, and vanilla extract and spoon a third of the mixture over the ladyfingers. Sprinkle with the remaining sugar, then spoon over half the remaining custard. Scatter with half the chopped chocolate, then spread with the remaining custard and sprinkle with the remaining chopped chocolate.

Chill for about 1 hour, until set. Serve dusted with unsweetened cocoa.

For raspberry tiramisu, put 1 cup raspberries in a pan with 1 tablespoon superfine sugar and 2 tablespoons water. Bring to a boil, remove from the heat, and beat with a wooden spoon to crush. Spoon into a strainer set over a bowl and press through the strainer to make a simple coulis. Prepare the other ingredients as above, omitting the coffee liqueur, and use the coulis to top the ladyfingers before layering the mascarpone and custard mixture. Add a layer of raspberries on top of the mascarpone. Sprinkle with cocoa to serve.

lemon & honeycomb pancakes

Serves **2**
Preparation time **6 minutes**
Cooking time **1–2 minutes**

½ cup **heavy cream**, plus
  extra to serve
1½ oz **sponge toffee**,
  crumbled
1 teaspoon finely grated
  lemon rind
¼ cup finely chopped **candied
  lemon peel** (optional)
⅓ cup traditional **lemon curd**
6 **pancakes**
blueberries, to serve

Combine the cream, sponge toffee, lemon rind,
candied lemon peel, if using, and lemon curd in a bowl.
Place a quarter of the lemon cream on a pancake, top
with a second pancake and another quarter of the
lemon cream on top, then finish with a third pancake.
Repeat the process so that you have 2 triple-decker
lemon pancakes.

Toast the pancake stacks in a sandwich grill for
1–2 minutes, or according to the manufacturer's
instructions, until the outside pancakes are toasted
and the lemon cream is beginning to ooze from the
sides. Serve immediately with some blueberries.

For blueberry & honey layers, mix 1 cup crème
fraîche (or ½ cup whipping cream mixed with ½ cup
sour cream) with 1 teaspoon finely grated lemon rind.
Make the pancakes as above. Spread lemon cream
over a pancake, sprinkle over a few blueberries, and
drizzle over some honey. Continue the layering,
finishing with a pancake. Drizzle with a little honey
to serve.

instant apple crumbles

Serves **4**

Preparation time **7 minutes**

Cooking time **13 minutes**

2 lb **Granny Smith apples**, peeled, cored, and thickly sliced

2 tablespoons **butter**

2 tablespoons **superfine sugar**

1 tablespoon **lemon juice**

2 tablespoons **water**

cream or **ice cream**, to serve

Crumble

4 tablespoons **butter**

1⅔ cups **fresh whole-wheat bread crumbs**

2 tablespoons **pumpkin seeds**

2 tablespoons **brown sugar**

Place the apples in a saucepan with the butter, sugar, lemon juice, and measured water. Cover and simmer for 8–10 minutes, until softened.

Melt the butter for the crumble in a skillet, add the bread crumbs, and stir-fry until lightly golden, then add the pumpkin seeds and stir-fry for an additional 1 minute. Remove from the heat and stir in the sugar.

Spoon the apple mixture into bowls, sprinkle with the crumble, and serve with cream or ice cream.

For instant pear & chocolate crumble, cook 2 lb pears in the butter, sugar, and water as above, adding ½ teaspoon ground ginger to the butter. Prepare the crumble as above, replacing the pumpkin seeds with 2 oz roughly chopped, dark chocolate. Cook as above.

chocolate millefeuilles

Serves **4**
Preparation time **10 minutes**
Cooking time **10 minutes**

1 lb 3½ oz **dark chocolate**,
  melted
7 oz **milk chocolate**, melted
8 oz **mascarpone cheese**
¾ cup **rasperries**
finely chopped **nuts**,
  to decorate

Spread a thin layer of melted chocolate onto a sheet of parchment paper. Drizzle more melted chocolate in a contrasting color over the top and feather the 2 chocolates together. Let stand until set but not brittle.

Cut into 3 inch squares, then let stand until brittle before peeling away the paper.

Layer the chocolate rectangles with spoonfuls of mascarpone and raspberries and sprinkle with some nuts to decorate.

For raspberry millefeuilles, use 1 lb 10 oz white chocolate to make the squares as above. Layer with cream and raspberries. Make a coulis by mixing 1 cup fresh raspberries with 1 teaspoon confectioners' sugar. Press the mixture through a strainer. Drizzle the coulis around the millefeuilles before serving.

layered sponge cake

Serves **8**
Preparation time **15 minutes**
Cooking time **20–25 minutes**

¾ cup (1½ sticks) **butter**, at
  room temperature, plus extra
  for greasing
¾ cup plus 2 tablespoons
  superfine sugar
3 **eggs**
1 teaspoon **vanilla extract**
1⅓ cups **self-rising flour**
1 teaspoon **baking powder**
3 tablespoons **strawberry
  preserve**
confectioners' sugar, to
  decorate

Put the butter and sugar in a mixing bowl and beat together with a wooden spoon until pale and creamy. Gradually beat in the eggs and vanilla extract, a little at a time, adding 1 tablespoon of flour with each addition, this will help to prevent the mixture from curdling.

Sift the remaining flour and baking powder into the bowl and fold gently into the creamed mixture.

Divide the mixture between two lightly oiled 7 inch sandwich pans that have been lined with a circle of wax paper or nonstick parchment paper. Spread the tops level, then bake in a preheated oven, 350°F, for about 20 minutes, or until the cake will spring back when lightly pressed with a fingertip. Let cool for 5 minutes, then loosen and turn the cakes out onto a wire rack, peel off the lining paper, and let cool.

Put one of the cakes, top downward onto a serving plate, spread with the preserve, then top with the second cake. Dust the top with sifted confectioners' sugar and cut into slices to serve.

For coffee & walnut cake, dissolve 3 tablespoons instant coffee in 2 tablespoons boiling water. Fold into the sponge mixture and bake as above. Make a coffee buttercream by beating together 2 cups confectioners' sugar, ½ cup (1 stick) softened unsalted butter, and 1 teaspoon instant coffee dissolved in 1 teaspoon boiling water until well blended and smooth. When the cakes are cool, spread the buttercream between the layers and scatter over ⅓ cup finely chopped walnuts. Dust with confectioners' sugar before serving.

pears with chocolate crumble

Serves **4**
Preparation time **5 minutes**
Cooking time **8 minutes**

¼ cup packed **light brown sugar**
⅔ cup **water**
25 g (1 oz) **raisins**
½ teaspoon **ground cinnamon**
4 ripe **pears**, peeled, halved and cored
3 tablespoons **unsalted butter**
⅔ cup **rolled oats**
¼ cup roughly chopped **hazelnuts**
2 oz **dark chocolate** or **milk chocolate**, chopped
lightly **whipped cream** or **Greek yogurt**, to serve (optional)

Place half of the sugar in a skillet or wide sauté pan with the measured water and the raisins and cinnamon. Bring just to a boil, add the pears, and simmer gently, uncovered, for about 5 minutes, until the pears are slightly softened.

Melt the butter in a separate skillet or saucepan. Add the rolled oats, and fry gently for 2 minutes. Stir in the remaining sugar and cook over a gentle heat until golden.

Spoon the pears onto serving plates. Stir the hazelnuts and chocolate into the oats mixture. Once the chocolate starts to melt, spoon over the pears. Serve topped with whipped cream or Greek yogurt, if desired.

For pan-fried oranges with chocolate crumble, use a serrated knife to cut the tops and bottoms from 4 oranges. Remove the rind and cut the oranges into thick slices. Heat 2 tablespoons butter in a skillet, add half the sugar and orange slices, and cook as above, omitting the water, raisins, and cinnamon. Make the crumble as above. Serve the warm pan-fried oranges with the chocolate crumble scattered over them.

chocolate chip cookies

Makes **25**
Preparation time **10 minutes**
Cooking time **15–20 minutes**

½ cup (1 stick) **butter**,
   softened, plus extra for
   greasing
¼ cup packed light **brown
   sugar**
1 **egg**, beaten
1¼ cups **self-rising flour**
4 oz **dark chocolate**, finely
   chopped

Grease a baking sheet lightly.

Put the butter and sugar in a mixing bowl and beat
together with a wooden spoon until light and fluffy.
Beat in the egg, then sift in the flour. Add the chocolate
pieces and mix thoroughly.

Put 25 teaspoonfuls of the mixture slightly apart
on the baking sheet and bake in a preheated oven,
350°F, for 15–20 minutes, until golden brown.

Remove from the oven and let stand on the baking
sheet for 1 minute, then transfer to a wire rack and
let cool.

For oatmeal & raisin cookies, mix the butter and
sugar as above. Add the egg and flour, replacing
¼ cup of the self-rising flour with ¼ cup rolled
oats. Add 1 teaspoon allspice to the flour. Omit the
chocolate but add generous ¼ cup raisins. Shape and
cook the dough as above and eat the cookies while
they are still warm.

quick hazelnut melts

Makes **20**
Preparation time **10 minutes**
Cooking time **15 minutes**

⅓ cup blanched **hazelnuts**
½ cup (1 stick) **butter**,
  softened, plus extra for
  greasing
¼ cup **superfine sugar**
1 ¼ cups **all-purpose flour**

Grind the hazelnuts in a food processor until fairly smooth, but still retaining a little texture. Dry-fry in a heavy skillet over low heat until evenly golden. Pour into a bowl and stir until cool.

Blend the butter and sugar together in the processor until creamy. Add the flour and cooled nuts and process again to make a soft dough.

Take walnut-size pieces of the dough and shape into rolls, then pat into flat ovals. Place on a greased baking sheet and bake in a preheated oven, 375°F, for 12 minutes, until just golden. Cool on a wire rack.

For chocolate & hazelnut creams, make 20 small cookies as above and let cool. Sandwich 2 cookies together using 1 teaspoon of chocolate-and-hazelnut spread between each. Serve lightly dusted with a little unsweetened cocoa for a real treat.

pineapple panettone sandwich

Serves **2**
Preparation time **4 minutes**
Cooking time **2–3 minutes**

4 **pineapple rings** in juice,
   drained
4 slices of **panettone**
¾ cup **miniature**
   marshmallows
⅓ cup crushed **macadamia**
   nuts
2 tablespoons **vanilla sugar**
confectioners' sugar, sifted,
   to decorate

Pat the pineapple rings dry on paper towels and arrange them on 2 slices of panettone. Scatter with the marshmallows and crushed macadamia nuts and sprinkle with the vanilla sugar. Top with the remaining 2 slices of panettone.

Toast in a sandwich grill for 2–3 minutes, or according to the manufacturer's instructions, until the bread is golden and the marshmallows are beginning to melt. Slice each sandwich into small rectangles and dust with confectioners' sugar. Serve immediately.

For apricot & ginger topped sandwiches, lightly toast one side of 4 slices of brioche. Drain 13 oz canned apricot halves and arrange the apricots on the untoasted side of 2 brioche slices. Place the slices on a broiler pan. Scatter over ⅓ cup crushed macadamia nuts and 1 finely chopped piece of preserved ginger. Sprinkle over the sugar and top with the other slices of brioche, untoasted side up, and broil for 2–3 minutes. Serve as above.

chocolate puddle pudding

Serves **4–6**
Preparation time **15 minutes**
Cooking time **15 minutes**

6 tablespoons **unsalted butter**, at room temperature
⅓ cup packed **light brown sugar**
3 **eggs**
½ cup **self-rising flour**
3 tablespoons **unsweetened cocoa**
½ teaspoon **baking powder**
confectioners' sugar, to decorate
ice cream or **cream**, to serve

Sauce

2 tablespoons **unsweetened cocoa**
¼ cup packed **light brown sugar**
1 cup boiling **water**

Rub a little of the butter all over the bottom and sides of an ovenproof dish and stand the dish on a baking sheet. Put the butter, sugar, and eggs in a large bowl and sift in the flour, unsweetened cocoa, and baking powder. Beat together with a wooden spoon until they form a smooth mixture. Spoon the pudding mixture into the dish and spread the top level.

Put the cocoa and sugar for the sauce into a small bowl and mix in a little of the measured boiling water to make a smooth paste. Gradually mix in the rest of the water, then pour the cocoa sauce over the pudding mixture.

Bake in a preheated oven, 350°F, for 15 minutes, or until the sauce has sunk to the bottom of the dish and the pudding is well risen. Sift a little confectioners' sugar over the pudding and serve with scoops of vanilla ice cream or a little cream.

For individual puddle puddings with orange cream,

prepare the mixture as above and spoon it into 4 lightly greased ramekins. Bake as above for 10–12 minutes, or until the puddings are well risen. Mix heavy cream with a little finely grated orange rind. Serve the warm puddings with a spoonful of the cream.

sabayon

Serves **4–6**
Preparation time **5 minutes**
Cooking time **5 minutes**

4 **egg yolks**
¼ cup **superfine sugar**
½ cup **dessert wine**
2 tablespoons **water**
thin shortbread cookies,
   to serve

Put all the ingredients in a heatproof bowl. Rest the bowl over a saucepan of gently simmering water, making sure that the bowl doesn't touch the water.

Beat the mixture using a handheld electric beater or balloon whisk for about 5 minutes, until it is very thick and foamy—the beaters or whisk should leave a trail when lifted from the bowl.

Remove the bowl from the heat and whisk for an additional 2 minutes. Spoon the sabayon into glasses or a warmed pitcher and serve immediately (it will collapse if left to stand) with thin shortbread cookies.

For zabaglione, a classic Italian dessert, make as above but use marsala in place of the dessert wine. Serve in glasses with cantuccini or biscotti to accompany.

index

acknowledgments

Executive Editor: Eleanor Maxfield
Senior Editor: Charlotte Macey
Executive Art Editor: Penny Stock
Designer: Barbara Zuniga
Photographer: Will Heap
Food Stylist: Sara Lewis
Prop Stylist: Rachel Jukes
Senior Production Controller: Carolin Stransky
Special Photography: © Octopus Publishing Group Limited/Will Heap

Other Photography: © Octopus Publishing Group/Stephen Conroy 12, 13, 43, 47, 51, 144, 221, 235; /David Jordan 53; /William Lingwood 29, 39, 119, 131, 167, 185, 205, 209, 227; /David Loftus 65; /David Munns 108; /Peter Myers 37; /Sean Myers 115, 135, 159, 175; /Lis Parsons 6, 10, 11, 54, 86, 176, 202, 217, 231; /William Reavell 69, 71, 127, 129, 165, 193, 199, 213, 225; /Simon Smith 19, 157; /Ian Wallace 16, 85, 121, 123, 137, 141, 229.